The Death of the Salesperson
Daniel Marshall

Dedicated to my girls,

Tanisha, for showing me the value of a daughter being proud of her father.

Ashlee, who always believes in me,

regardless of her own fears.

Angelice, for teaching me to love what you cannot hold.

And to my wife Nici,

for her continued encouragement, and understanding.

The Death of the Salesperson
Copyright © Daniel Marshall 2014

Daniel Marshall has asserted his right to be the author of this work.

All rights reserved.

No part of this publication may be reproduced or transmitted by any person or entity, including internet search engines or retailers, in any form or by any means, electronic or mechanical, including photocopying (except under the statutory exceptions provisions of the Australian Copyright Act 1968), recording, scanning or by any information storage and retrieval system without the prior written permission of Lulu Publishing.

Cataloguing-in-Publication Entry
Author: Daniel Marshall
Title: The Death of the Salesperson
ISBN: 978-1-326-01213-7
Target Audience: Business, Sales & Marketing

ID: 15218031
www.lulu.com

Contents

ABOUT THE AUTHOR		9
DEATH		1
INTRODUCTION		3
1	DON'T TAKE NOTES	9
2	TRUST ME	17
3	OLD SCHOOL THAT STILL WORKS	26
4	DON'T BEAT-EM JOIN-EM	31
5	WE NEED LOYAL CUSTOMERS, NOT HAPPY CUSTOMERS.	33
6	TRANSFER THIS!	37
7	EXPERIENCE IS USELESS	41
8	DON'T FOLLOW UP TO GET A SALE	46
9	DON'T ASK FOR THE SALE MORE THAN ONCE	52
10	FEAR THE REAPER	55
11	WHAT ARE WE FIGHTING FOR?	59

12	WHAT'S THE PROBLEM	65
13	ARE YOU UNIQUE?	69
14	DON'T BE THE SMARTEST PERSON IN THE ROOM	72
15	THE DEVIL'S ADVOCATE	74
16	BARGAINING	77
17	SET A GOAL FOR YOURSELF, NOT A BUDGET	80
18	A GOAL MAY NOT BE ENOUGH	83
19	SET A SALES GOAL FOR YOUR CUSTOMERS	87
20	YOUR NOT AS IMPORTANT AS THEY ARE	89
21	IT ISN'T NUMBERS GAME	94
22	WHY SHOULD THEY BUY FROM YOU	99
23	DON'T OVERCOME OBJECTIONS	102
24	NOT EVERYONE CAN SELL	107
25	DON'T GO STRAIGHT FOR THE RELATIONSHIP	109
26	WHAT CAN YOU DO FOR ME	112

27	USE YESTERDAY'S IDEAS TODAY, AND YOU'LL BE BROKE TOMORROW	114
28	SALES AND MARKETING ARE ONE IN THE SAME	116
29	DON'T BE THE HARDEST WORKING PERSON IN THE OFFICE	119
30	TALK ABOUT FAILURE.	121
31	WHAT DO YOU DO	124
32	THE DEATH OF (TRADITIONAL) MARKETING	126
33	TIME IS MONEY?	129
34	THE NEW WAY	133
	Marketing.	134
	Interest.	135
	Need.	135
	Insight.	135
	Reason.	136
	Accurate.	137
	Plan.	137
	Solution.	138
35	CONCLUSION	139

About the author

I was only twelve years old when I realized how rewarding the sales industry, could be. Our school was having a fundraiser for the Children's hospital. The deal was to sell vouchers for a raffle of a car. For most people this was a good thing.
Donate and have a chance to win something in the same instance. For the door knockers like me, there was an added advantage. For every voucher we sold we would receive a credit to our name, and the more vouchers you sold, the more credits. At the end of the raffle drive we would have the opportunity to cash in all our credits for rewards, rewards like toys, radios and even bikes.
Well this was more than an opportunity to me, this was a career. While all the other kids where at home watching Ninja Turtles, (I'm so happy they're back by the way) I was out door knocking. I didn't even focus on the rewards, sure that was a cool thing to look forward to, but what really drove me was the challenge, the milestones to reach each prize and to beat the other kids. To win and to keep on keeping on despite being given a "no" by some of the people I prospected. Without any training whatsoever, I was the king of selling. I was the number one in our school, not by a margin, but by ten times the next person. No skills, no tactics, just plain old drive and determination. I averaged a 90% success rate. I know this because the boom box I won was worth one thousand credits, there was only a population of five hundred people in my home town of Gembrook, most people only wanted one or two tickets and the tickets were worth 1 credit each.

Then came the flip side. In my later years I had a similar opportunity with the MS Readathon. Read some books, get some donations and get a bunch of prizes. But by the time I hit sixteen, something was different. I no longer had the ability to sell to the masses. I was the same and the drive I had to win was the same, but I remember having trouble for the first several weeks. The same thing would happen night after night. I would door knock for an hour, following a carefully planned script that was provided by the foundation. Then after several rejections I would lose heart and call it a night. Then I remember after three weeks of doing this, I visited a friend's house in Avonsleigh, near our school. His mum answered the door and I went through my pitch. My mate Steve heard me at the door and came running up to see me. He said "Danny, what the hell are you doing, I thought you were someone else, you sounded different". It was at Steve's house I realized in an instant what I was doing wrong. I was following a planned out sales pitch that was designed for the amateur. I sir, was a professional. The very next night I went out in to the market with a new plan, not to have a preconceived sales pitch. I would just do what I did before I knew any better. I just started to talk to people.

"My names Daniel, may I have a moment of your time" became "Hi, that dinner smells good, I'm doing the readathon, sorry, Daniel, I've got, three tickets left. Your neighbor James bought the rest".

I remember the change and what a difference it made. I know some of you are thinking, "Should have made the pitch your own" well I say get rid of it all together. We have heard them all and every variation of it.

Over the years, I had lots of other exposures to this chain of thought. In my twenties I worked for a real-estate agent who loved the sales tactics and strategies, and all I ever did was made a point of chatting to the neighbors when I was putting up a 'for sale' sign in my overalls. I always did better doing that than the guys in the office who door knocked and cold called.

In my early thirties, I worked as a sales rep for a pneumatics company. I learnt then the value of being the one to offer insight and knowledge to find the problem and solve it, verses someone who just keeps selling products to the customer until they have either had enough and moved on to a competitor or fixed the problem by a costly trial and error.

I have been in the sales industry for over fifteen years. In that time I have seen what works, what does not work, and what will get you at best, told they will think about it, and at worst, thrown out of the building.

This is not a book written by someone who has studied sales and marketing at uni, then decided to share what they have read via cut and paste. This is a book written by someone who has tried and tested these sales principles in the field. From selling daffodils, to video games, and real-estate.

For seven years I have owned and operated a successful amusement center and Laundromat. I have been a telemarketer for a year, and a vending machine operator for five years whilst selling solar panels for houses.

This is but a brief history of my life and the only reason I am sharing this with you is not to try and impress you, but rather impress upon you the diverse sales experiences I have accumulated. Add to this the dozens of sales books and audio I have studied for a basis comparison and to pick the cherries off.

Keep in mind that any and in fact all of the ideas here are just that, ideas, and should be considered, run with, altered or dropped at your best judgment. I am merely spilling my guts, and some of you won't like the look of it.

Death

The act of dying; the end of life; the total and permanent cessation of all the vital functions of an organism.

"Nothing lasts forever, nothing is permanent, but where there is death, there is always new life"

Salesperson

A person who sells merchandise or services either in a shop or by canvassing in a designated area.

"I'd be a really good salesman if I wasn't so caring, honest and moral"

Introduction

The world of selling has changed. It has changed because the world of buying changed first. A twelve year old girl with a smart phone will now have access to more information in the palm of her hands, than the president of the United States did twenty years ago.

A salesperson will never be able to compete with this, so the tables have turned and now technology, has done away with the need for a face to face type of communication people used to need, in order to get what they want.

One can, and indeed some do, live an entire existence without leaving their home. We can find a product, compare prices and quality, research all the pros and cons, read others reviews and then make a much more educated purchase in our pajamas than if we had gone to the shops.

Salespeople, whoa whoa, whoa, what are we good for.

So if we are not really needed, what have the sales people of the world become in the last twenty or so years.

Today a professional salesperson is not the stereotyped suede jacket bow tie snake oil seller or the fast talking gold chains Hawaiian shirt and crocodile skin booted used car salesman we have come to know and love. Those sales people are as historic as cassette tapes and denim jackets. We are now looking for a new breed of sales professional, in fact we are not even looking for sales people at all, what we need is something entirely different.

Several years ago we decided to sell our house, and so we called a couple of real estate agents. The first was honest and down to earth. He said we could get $275,000 for the house and told us we may have to be patient with the sale of this one and advised us to spend some time and money on the place. The second agent was the one who had all the tricks we have come to love in salesmen. I believed him when he said he will get a price higher than the market was offering, and we believed him when he said the market was strong. He said he had a list of the names of people waiting for a house just like the one we had, and if we signed up with him today we were sure to get the sale for well over $300,000 and we believed that too. After all, why wouldn't we believe him?

So of course we signed up with the second agent.

Is this beginning to sound familiar to you?

Well as it turned out, no less than a week later, agent number two called us to say he needed to see us and can he come around tonight. To our naïve surprise he turned up with a signed contract, with an offer of exactly $275,000. Now how about that, it was spot on to the amount agent number one told us he could get. I asked the agent number two why he would go to the trouble of getting a signed offer for less than he said he could get. No answer, no real answer any way. We promptly told him to go off and get upwards of $300,000 and don't come back to us with a signed offer unless we agree to one verbally. Of course now we know this to be a tactic called 'high siding'. Where agents will deliberately claim they can get you a higher sell price for a house, and then come back to you with an offer much less, or the market value to see if you bite. In fact as it turns out, a lot of people do sell at that lower price.

The initial high sided offer is just to get the listing. The turning up a week later with a signed offer, is like waving a bone in front of a hungry dog. We were wanting to sell, and he was just hoping we really wanted to sell. If you have ever bought and sold a property, then you will most probably have a story like this one. You may even have a similar one from white goods salesman or a car yard. My point is we have all been burnt by a slimy salesperson full of tactics and strategies that only serve to make us aware of the situation in the future. To use an extreme example, let's say you have just received an email like the following one.

Good Day,

My name is Dr William Monroe, a staff in the Private Clients Section of a well-known bank, here in London, England. One of our accounts, with holding balance of £15,000,000 (Fifteen Million Pounds Sterling) has been dormant and last operated three years ago. From my investigations and confirmation, the owner of the said account, a foreigner by name John Shumejda died on the 4th of January 2002 in a plane crash in Birmingham.

Since then, nobody has done anything as regards the claiming of this money, as he has no family member that has any knowledge as to the existence of either the account or the funds; and also Information from the National Immigration also states that he was single on entry into the UK.

I have decided to find a reliable foreign partner to deal with. I therefore propose to do business with you, standing in as the next of kin of these funds from the deceased and funds released to you after necessary processes have been followed.

This transaction is totally free of risk and troubles as the fund is legitimate and does not originate from drug, money laundry, terrorism or any other illegal act.

On your interest, let me hear from you URGENTLY.

Best Regards,
Dr William Monroe Financial Analysis and Remittance Manager
[Phone Number Removed]

Would you continue to communicate with this person? Of course you wouldn't, even though chances are you have never seen the email before as it is one of many hundreds in circulation, you can see the very nature of the email is shady. The first few lines are usually enough to make most of us shake our fist at the computer screen click delete, and move on to the next email.

So how do we know deep down we need to avoid it? Why are we so aware of this Nigerian scam type email? We know it's a scam because we live in the Information Age, and just as easy as it is for the scammers to send out this email to you, so is it easy for you yourself to send an email to the world, warning friends and family of the threat. We see it on TV and we read it in the news, all the stories and tales of peoples little tricks, tactics and scams. All in the name of taking our hard earned cash.

Now I know the shady real-estate agent I mentioned before is just doing what he figures he needs to do to be an effective real-estate agent in a competitive market, and I was never going to lose my life savings and go to jail for international fraud by dealing with him, but I'm sure you can understand that after several dealings with them, and a few bad eggs is all it takes, I now look at an agent with squinty eyes wondering what he is going to say next to get my signature.

Unfortunately used car salesmen have the same stigma, as do the good old telemarketer. I'm sure there was a time when, if someone called you and offered you a better deal on your electricity you may have sat down and listened to them, but those days are no more.

Whether we fall for them or not, we do not trust those rehearsed in the art of emptying our pockets. We are learning more and more every day on how to spot the lines and phrases that are the tricks of the trade, so when we hear someone say something like "wouldn't you agree that's a good price" or "if you sign up right now" we get a shiver down our spine that tells us we are about to be had.

So what if you are a salesperson, what now? How do we master the art of sales, when the world is mastering the art of sales-defense?

Let me put it real simple right now. As the title of the book suggests, the salesperson is dead. Shot down, dead in the water, at peace, assumed room temperature, has fifteen minutes of flame, pushing up daisies, six feet under and bought the farm.

Unfortunately, most people in sales do not know this.

Unfortunately for them that is, because once you know the salesman is indeed gone out with ones tie on and kicked the bucket, then you can be done with all the strategies and tactics that make the world throw up on you. You can begin to build yourself in to a respectable, admirable product manager, consultant, or service manager and start looking after people instead of trying to sell to them, because as the great communicator Zig Ziglar says "help enough others get what they want and you will eventually get what you want."

In this book I will show you what used to work and is still being unsuccessfully practiced. I will show you how to care for and guide people through what is usually a very scary process of buying goods and services of high value, and I will also go through a few old school methods that still work.

The foundation to this book is to build trust with people. Trust is first and foremost. If you have people's genuine trust they will come back to you time and time again. Indeed they will send others to you as referrals and your business will naturally grow. Without trust, you will fight for sales your entire career. Some you will win, but it will be hard work and you will have to do it again and again, so if you feel like you are working too hard to get the sales you need, then I'm sorry to say this to you, people don't trust you. Actually I'm not really sorry, it's rather funny imagining the look on the faces of all you untrusted folks. You are not trusted and that is that. Finished.

But not for long, because you can learn how to become honest and trustworthy and I will show you how, even if you sell TVs to people you interact with for ten minutes you can build trust. So throw out the tie and briefcase and get ready for a change in how customers see you and how you see yourself, we are going to build you from a salesman or woman in to, my good honest friend, and consultant who sells stuff.

1 Don't take notes

The old school will tell you to take a diary in to every meeting and take all the necessary notes. The new professional way is to simply remember. I know what you're thinking, well I don't really but, I'm guessing you think remembering all the meetings details will be tough, now I said simply remember, not easily.

If you think there is no way you could ever remember the important stuff, then indulge me for this little experiment.

Imagine for a moment, you walk in to a prospective clients office and shake hands with them as they introduce themselves as Arnold, and you immediately think of Arnold Schwarzenegger holding a machine gun in one hand, a cigar between his teeth while giving you an arm-wrestle handshake predator style. The prospect tells you he loves hiking, you imagine him with a backpack walking up a winding trail, and he loves hiking with his two sons, Jack aged ten and Tom aged twelve, you imagine two young boys hiking one holding a jack in the box continually winding it till it pops out with a big number ten on a spring, and one boy on the shoulders of Tom Hanks holding a dozen chocolates talking about life and such.

> *How many objects or things do you think you can remember at a time?*

Now, without looking back, what's the name of your prospect?

His favorite past time?

And his boys names?

What about their ages?

Chances are, if you remembered them now, you will remember them in a week and a month. The better the visualization, the better the memory. When someone tells you their name, attempt an association of that person's name with someone you already know of and can picture and picture them doing the things they tell you. Just give it a go next time you meet someone.

This book is not a memory book by any means, so I am just giving you a little kick start because I have found it to be a necessary tool in every day sales, and then I suggest you put memory training down as part of your self-improvement program.

In this book I will teach you an abundance of methods and lessons to help you to become a great sales professional. It is all too much to take in within a short period of time, that time being the time it takes you to read this book. Using a system called the linking system, you will be able to retain a vast majority of the golden nuggets that is contained within these pages, simply by reading them once. If used regularly, you will no longer need to take notes for customer orders and product lists.

The reason I am using such a system this early in the book, is because there is so much to learn and I believe this to be the best way to retain all the chapters that follow.

Once you know this system, you can, and you most likely will want to use this system every day of your life, to remember everything from shopping lists to jobs to do, to the ingredients of a recipe. I use this system in every day work life, for mental lists and customer product orders.

The linking system is linking or associating one thing to another by creating an image of the two together.

If you learn by this association and you do it well, you will understand and retain far more and for much longer than by just being told.

Let me show you what I mean.

How many objects or things do you think you can remember at a time?

If I gave you a list of things to remember, how big would I be able to make that list, five things? Six things? Maybe even ten things you can recall of a list, for a while.

How long would you think you could remember it accurately?

Ten minutes, an hour at best.

I will now show you a method for remembering things that I will use throughout this book.

This method is a big bonus to you because it's simply good to know it.

You will be able to remember a list as long as you like. Ten, twenty, even thirty plus objects. Not only that, you will remember them in a week from now, a month from now and even a year from now, if you chose to.

It's called the Linking System.

The linking system is simply this, associate one thing with the next and then the next and so on, creating a visual, meaningful link as we go.

Let's start with these twelve items. Go ahead and read them out loud. If you are in a public place, pretend you are on the phone.

Car
Book
Dog
Tree
Milk
Bed
Shoe
Grass
Hammer
Socks
Penguin
Shower

Now, close the book and try to recall all of them.

Did you try to remember them all?

How did you go?

If you could remember all of them then you do not need to know what I am about to show you. If you struggled, then pay attention.

The Linking System

Try to visualize each of these links that I have made for you here.

Truly picture this in your head. The better you can imagine the image the easer you will be able to remember the list. In fact after each linked two items close your eyes for a moment and get a concrete image, and don't move on till you do have that image.

The rules for this system are simple.

The image must be vivid, you need to truly see the picture in your mind.

It must be unusual, just having a cup full of water if you are trying to remember cup and water is too common and normal, something like a cup made of water just magically staying in the shape of a cup.

Finally it must be a definite connection to the two items. A duck in a wig shop, although funny, needs more connection. It must be wearing the wig, or imagine a wig looking like a duck.

Let me show you what I have come up with for the list of items.

We will now link the first item, Car, to the second, Book.

Picture a car made entirely out of books. The doors the roof, driving on book wheels, even the engine is a rumbling pile of books. Every time you attempt to open the door, you just keep turning the massive pages and the bonnet flies open and all the bonnet book pages flip when you get up to speed on the road.

From Book, to Dog.

I picture a big yellow Labrador digging in to a pile of books as big as a house. Book flying out from under his scratching paws like they were being catapulted off a conveyor line he digs and he digs, only to find a book he has been searching for, a book on bones.

From Dog, to Tree.

They say dogs don't grow on trees, well I don't know who says that but anyway. I see a tree covered in ripe Chiwawas, Alsatians and Beagles. Some kicking, others scratching and a few just dangling from their branches asleep, all ripe and ready for the picking.

From Tree to Milk.

With cows now extinct, we must extract the sap from trees as a milk supplement. Luckily scientists have engineered a tree that has milk for sap, simply cut a branch and the milk will pour from it like water from a tap.

From Milk to Bed.

Ever sleep in a waterbed? Well how about a milk bed, better yet, a bed made of milk, you lie down in a small bed full of milk like a little pool. The warm milk covers over you like a milk blanket, and this sends you straight off to sleep, only to have dreams of drinking milk on a cow flying in the Milky Way.

From Bed to Shoe.

Picture yourself trying to walk down the street, with single beds tied to your feet, instead of shoes. You can only seem to drag them from one to the other you move at a slow pace. This is not at all what you might call resting your feet.

From Shoe to Grass.

You have seen shoes made of grass, but have you ever seen grass made of shoes? Imagine an entire front lawn made of trimmed green growing shoes. All different colors and sizes, and when the sun comes out, the tongues curl back and the shoes blossom

From Grass to hammer.

 I have invented a new type of lawn mower, made of a dozen smashing hammers hanging out like fingers on a keyboard; dozens of hammers smash, bash and whack the grass in to submission.

Hammer to Socks.

Instead of ironing your socks (well fine maybe you don't then), picture taking to them with a sledge hammer, over and over to really get those wrinkles out, and destroying the ironing board in the process.

Socks to Penguin.

You have seen the little slippers that resemble penguins, well I wear penguins on my feet as slippers. They are warm, soft and they squeak as I walk, get a bit nippy sometimes though.

From Penguin to Shower.

You walk in to a shower room at your local gymnasium, to your surprise you see several standing, singing penguins under each shower, ten of them, shampooing, washing and singing. You walk up to one and politely ask if they are nearly done as you would like to use the shower. A quick squeak and a sqwak and they turn off the tap and move aside.

Now, if you have really made an effort to picture these items and their weird links then I would like you to attempt again to recall the twelve items. Go on, and write them down. See how you went with visualizing them, the first one is Car.

So how did you go?

Give yourself a pat on the back if you truly deserve it. You can use this as a party trick, for a mental product list whilst you're driving, or to remember points of a presentation.

All you have to really know is three things

Make it strange and unusual, so it will make an impression in your head.

Make a solid link between the two items you are linking.

Feel the emotion behind the link. What I mean by that is, if it's funny laugh at it. If it is sad feel the sadness. If it's gross, feel a bit grossed out by it.

Make a strange link, visualize it, feel it and move to the next one.

Follow this system and you will be able to recall lists as big as you like.

At the end of each chapter I'll have a 'Remember' word to help you retain the chapter's message.

2 Trust Me

The traditional sales mentality is that of talking people in to a sale, using sales pitches, convincing arguments and rehearsed carefully planned sales scripts to pressure or gain a sort of confidence. Essentially, this is just the stuff of a confidence man or, con-man. This old way of, act now and get a free set of steak knives died in the eighties. Unfortunately the late night infomercials don't know it yet.
But wait there's more (sorry). If we go down this path of only focusing on openers' sales pitches and closes, we will never build a successful sales business, where you are the one people look for when they think of the product or service you sell. We would have to work and work hard at each sale, making us feel like the trickster at the circus having to spin the plates on a stick to stop them crashing to the floor.
Trust is the beginning. Without your customers trusting in you there is no relationship, and if there is no relationship, all you are doing is working to convince them of the value of your product or service. The Latin root of convince is *convincere*. Con- meaning to and Vincere meaning conquer. That doesn't sound like the sort of thing I want to do to people.

When people trust you they put their faith in what you are saying whether they understand it or not. They believe YOU, even if they do not believe in what you are selling. People will take a leap of faith just because it is you who is the one telling them it's ok. When people trust you, you become the giant they need, the expert they need and the leader they need to guide them through right choices to make.

There was once a little red hen. Every morning she would wake up, lay one egg and wander over to a nearby river, where she could see on the other side, there was a wonderful field of vegetables and berries Sadly the little hen could not reach the other side, because she was a chicken, and chickens cannot swim or fly very well at all. One day she saw a salesman (actually it was a snake, but this works). The salesman said "I have a magnificent red boat made of wood and nails. I will give you free ores and you can get to the other side of the river with it, if you give me ten eggs, I will give you the boat". So the hen, thinking this was a great deal, returned to her hen house and gathered her savings of eggs. She handed them over, and the salesman gave her the boat. But there was a problem. You see a hen has only small wings and so they cannot row a boat. "Well that was a waste of good eggs" she said, and she went back to the hen house and back to laying eggs. A few weeks later, another salesman was passing by, and saw the hen staring longingly at the field on the other side of the river. The salesman said to the hen "I have a wonderfully long rope you could use to swing to the other side of the river with. For ten eggs, I will give you this beautiful rope". Now the hen was a little more careful this time. And she decided to ask a few more questions. "How will I tie it?" she asked "well you can get to that branch and tie it on" this was true, she could reach the lower branches and tie the rope with her feet. "How will I hold the rope to swing?" she asked "you can swing over with your beak holding the rope" said the salesman.

So the hen, believing all her doubts where resolved, gave the salesman ten eggs and took the rope. She flapped up to the highest branch she could reach and tied it to the tree, then flapped back to the ground. Then picking up the end of the rope in her beak, the little hen backed up for a running start. She ran and flapped and ran and jumped off the river bank, the rope went tight and she could feel herself flying through the air. Flying and swinging, until, splash. In the middle of the river. It was all she could do to keep afloat, let alone get back to the riverbank, chickens are not good swimmers. The rope would not carry her all the way across the river, and the little hen almost drowned. Never wishing to see a salesman again, the little hen went back to her house and back to her job of laying eggs. As the weeks and months went on, several more salesmen offered her many things to get across the river. One even offered her a motorcycle to jump over! In the hens eyes all salesmen want is to sell things to her. One summer's day, several months later, the little hen was visiting another farm and saw a farmer building a wooden thing over another river. When she asked the other hens what it was, they told her it was called a bridge, and they will use it to cross the river safely, and with that the little hen went back to the hen house and began looking on the henternet (asking other animals) for how to build a bridge. She researched and she researched, all night and all day, until she knew more than anyone about bridges. The little hen was sitting at the river bank wondering about all the many ways there was to build a bridge. Would she use steel like the city ones or concrete like the road ones? As the little hen was sitting on the river bank, an owl flew down and sat beside her. "I hear you are wanting to build a bridge?" said the owl. "If you're a salesman, I'm fine and I need nothing from you" said the hen. "Oh but I'm no salesperson" exclaimed the owl "I'm a bridge consultant". "A consultant?" questioned the hen. "I should suggest you not use concrete as the banks are too weak and the steel is too costly for a small bridge like this one" for the next three days the consultant advised the little hen on all the things she needed to consider for a bridge. The hen liked the owl consultant, and because he was willing to listen to her and tell her the right thing to do for her, she trusted the owl. Some weeks later and under the guidance of the owl consultant, little hen began to build a perfect wooden bridge. The hen didn't care that the bridge cost more than the boat and the rope put together. She loved that the consultant returned once a month to see how her lovely bridge was going, and every time he did, she gave him a bag of vegies from the field half a dozen eggs, and a list of names of others looking to build things.

What you are to people who trust you, screams so loud, they can't hear what you are saying to them.

Focus on gaining trust and the rest will be a downhill run.

Ok so how do we get the customers to trust us then?

In the story, the Owl used his knowledge. He knew everything there was to know about bridges, and he knew what would work for the Hen.

It comes down to these two things,

Know your business, and know theirs.

There is nothing worse than a sales person trying to sell you something they themselves have very little knowledge of, actually there is. A salesperson trying to sell you something you don't need or cannot use. In this case the customer would either have to educate the salesperson on either what they are selling, or on the customers own businesses requirements. The salesperson's credibility will be long gone, and at best, recover enough to move on with a better understanding of what they are doing with the next customer.

Imagine you are going for an evening walk and you come across a person on the dark footpath you are walking on. They are on their hands and knees brushing their hands over the ground as if to be looking for something. You approach the person and ask them if they need help. They tell you they are looking for their gold watch on the ground, they are sure it is here somewhere because this is where they felt it fall off. If you would help them, they tell you they would be so grateful as to give you fifty bucks. So you tell them it's too dark here on the foot path. Let's go over to the well-lit shopping center where we can see better to look for the watch.

The person on their hands and knees is your customer and you the helper is offering them part of a solution that will not help them at all.

We have learned their problem but we need to truly understand the full picture. The real solution is to get a torch or lamp and bring it to the site. As funny as this story sounds, I see it every day with sales people. They hear a problem without really listening and offer a fix that will not really solve their problem.

At the time of writing this book, my sister is trying to sell her house. The agent (I'm not trying to pick on real-estate agents, they are just so dammed funny) they first used advised them of a price they were happy with and listed it at that price. So far so good. A few months later there was a little interest but still no sale. So the agent suggested the only thing the bad agents (not the ones reading this book) do and told them they should lower the price. They thanked him for his efforts, and set the dogs on to him. They then called an agent a friend had recommended to them. When he arrived, the first thing he said was "paint that wall, change those curtains and fix that path, then give me a call and I'll get your asking price. Until then I will not list this house for what you are asking". He knew he was at risk of losing the sale to another agent, but he wanted to do right by them and be honest about what needed to happen. Currently they are doing just what he suggested they do with the greatest of intention of calling him when they are done.

> *Learn your product or service better than the next person and the one after them. Study the industry with an intention of being the best in your field.*

He listened to what they wanted and risked his listing to show them the way to get it. He knew the industry and the market so well, he knew what had to happen for them to get their price.

Learn your product or service better than the next person and the one after them. Study the industry with an intention of being the best in your field. Who owns who, when it was founded and the person who invented it. Strive to know more than anyone you sell to, indeed strive to know more than anyone in the same office as you and your competitors office. If you sell a product, study the manufacture of that product and the process required to get it to your customer. All its uses, advantages and disadvantages. If you sell a service, learn what its origin is and how long has it been in existence for. Are there better ways of doing it? Go to seminars and trade shows.

Do a cradle to grave map for yourself.

A cradle to grave map is simply a beginning to end of your product or service, so if you are selling a product, track it right back to its raw materials, and I mean out of the ground raw. Where was it mined and refined? Where was it processed and built? What did that process look like? Even talk to the head of manufacturing if you can. This is great if you work for an international business to really close the gap, "Frank is our head of operations in Sweden, really thorough bloke, and loves to fish" .Who shipped it to you? All manner of technical details need to be investigated, because If you are meeting with a prospect who is extremely concerned about the environment, and asks you if your products are made with forest killing materials, or environmentally unfriendly processes and you don't have an answer for them, it may be the death of the sale. On the other hand if you have an intelligent answer for them, even if it is not the one they are looking for, the credibility you gain in knowing your own business may just save you. Learn your business. If nothing more, it's professional.

Know their business.

Study their ups and downs, how long they have been trading and who founded them. Study what they do, how and why they do it. Their company mission statement. Phone them as a prospect yourself just to see their sales process.
Learn their demographics, and who will buy from them. Who are they looking to expand to?
Are you dealing with a business in a service that has a short interaction time like a home appliance shop or one of those walk in massage parlors we see in shopping centers? If so then learn the demographics of who will be walking through the door or their competitors' door. Understanding your customer's customers will get you a level of respect you will not be able to get any other way. It's like giving advice to parent on how to raise her kids, when you have never met her kids, versus someone who has known her kids very well all their lives giving educated advice. Use the same cradle to grave principle you used in gaining knowledge of your own business to build knowledge of their business.
Rudy Nielsen, founder of NIHO (Nielsen Holdings) committed years of his life to go from losing almost everything to becoming one of the world's greatest recreational real-estate agents by dedicating himself to learning everything there is to know about the land he sells.

Know the industry and internal business problems before you meet them. If you can tell them what the problem is before they tell you they will treat you like a doctor who has found an illness. They will ask you to help them fix the problem.

*A little girl and her father were crossing a bridge.
The father was a little scared so he asked his little daughter,
'Sweetheart, please hold my hand,
so that you don't fall into the river.'
The little girl said,
'No, Dad. You hold my hand.'
'What's the difference?'
Asked the puzzled father.
'There's a big difference,'
replied the little girl.
'If I hold your hand and something happens to me,
chances are that I may let your hand go.
But if you hold my hand, I know for sure that no matter what
happens, you will never let my hand go.'*

In any relationship, the essence of trust is not in its bind, but in its bond. So go out and hold the hand of the customer rather than expecting them to hold yours...

They may not know they need you until you take their hand and show them the unforeseen dangers or failings they may come across.

Build trust, with knowledge, and homework.

Remember

Trust.

3   Old school that still works

Humans learn from humans. We study other people and follow what they have learnt. That's what we do, in fact that is really all we do. We have very little natural instinct. We can feed and procreate though we still have plenty of education on the two of those. Left to our own devices, with a minimum amount of communication with others and we would cease to learn and evolve. As is the case with most every indigenous tribe around the world. Nothing new learnt, and nothing new passed on. For tens of thousands of years in some cases. But when we travel to new and exotic places, we will inadvertently discover new things, learn new skills and pass on this new found knowledge to family and friends.

In my early twenty's I set off to see one of the world's most amazing manmade structures, The Great Wall of China.

Within the first five minutes of arriving in Beijing I was being had. From the overpriced taxi driver who charged me ten times what I should have paid, because I sir, had the good taxi. To the bars that turned out to be pay per view karaoke bars, I'll get back to that one. I would like to tell you about the best guilty close I have ever seen. Say what you want about a communist country, these people are more capitalist than I will ever be.

We arrived at the base of a long walk to the main guard tower that would be our starting point for a five kilometer Great Wall hike. The moment we got off the bus we were met by two young women who took our bags and begun walking with us. Assuming they were part of the tour group we let them carry the back packs and began taking photos on the way up the hill. It wasn't a steep hill nor was the road long but it was a hot day and those girls kept a good pace, to ensure a decent sweat would appear upon their brow. Twenty minutes later we had arrived. Our packs where placed neatly on the ground and there in front of us, two little sets of hands were outstretched before bowed heads, enter 'The Guilty Close'. With a sigh for being had again I said drearily "How much then?" "Jus pay wha you wan" said one of the girls, still puffing. And of course being a wealthy Australian man (not) we paid them much more than they would have earned working for a wage where the average is $35 a day. We saw this technique many times in China, most of all where there were lots of stupid tourists to be had, like us. No one really minded though, fair work for fair pay and all that. We see this same 'guilty close' in our lives back home as well, and we all fall for it, even you.

Ever donated to a tin rattler. Or paid a man to do what your car's wiper blades do for free. What about this one I fell for only a few months ago.

I get a knock at the door at home one evening.

When I answer it, I am greeted by a respectable looking teenaged girl.

Door knocker girl; "hello I'm from the starlight foundation."

Me; "what's a starlight foundation? Do you harness the power of the sun and the stars to use it for all kinds of good in the world?"

Door knocker girl; "Harness what?"

My joke being completely lost on her, she begins to describe the many tragic stories of all the children on their death beds in the royal children's hospital, whilst showing me the matching photos of the children in their hospital beds.

After about three or four examples of sick and terminal kids, she promptly takes out a receipt book and says "would you help us with a donation?"

Nice!

This age old close still does and will forever have its place in our society, as long as we continue to have a conscience but unless you have a genuine sob story, this one isn't going to do too well for you, and even then, some people have been exposed to this a thousand times and just don't care anymore.

The second greatest close I have seen took place even after I thought I had my ammunition.

This one begins with me doing what I thought to be my due diligence in researching the best for my family in the latest and greatest technology that never really seemed to take off, Blu-Ray. Why didn't it become the next best thing in tech I wonder? Anyway, the Blu-Ray had been released. We had ourselves a disc from a kindly relative Christmas gift and now all we needed was a player. All night I researched. Ones with USBs, some with networking and others that recorded on to hard drive, and I learnt the correct prices for all of these features. I had my knowledge, knowledge is power, and so I was all powerful.

> *Be careful with the assumptive close. It is only for the indecisive ones who have a hard time saying "yes, I'll take that one"*

We arrived at the shopping center, I dutifully handed a tenner to the kids, and the good wife took the rest as she regularly attempts to replicate the scene from the eighties cartoon intro to The Jetsons'. You know where he hands her the money, and she takes his wallet and… never mind.

I went to the electronics store and begun my eyeing-off the stock, checking their teeth and hoofs so to speak. Within a few minutes a smart looking bloke comes up to me. Here we go I say to myself. I'm in sales now so I'm not having some young buck telling me what I'm going to buy. This is how it goes down.

"Hello, are you looking to get a Blu-Ray player?" "Why yes" I say. "It needs a USB and Wi-Fi ability." "Will this one do?" he says pointing to a shiny black box. "Well sure but it's a bit pricey" I say. So he offers another "and this has the features you want and the price you are happy with?" "well yes and it's the right price range I say" and with that he snaps it off the shelf and takes it to the counter without another word spoken, me skipping along behind him index finger in the air as if to have a question, wondering what just happened to me. I, had been Assumptive Closed. This situation called for it and it worked. It was unlikely I would ever see him again and he knew it. The worst that would have happened is me stopping him. This is a risky close and if done wrong, you won't make any friends, in fact it can come across as pushy to some, but in very few instances, where both you and the customer knows it's the correct choice, perhaps the Assumptive Close is the one to go for. Again be careful with it though. It is only for the indecisive ones who have a hard time saying "yes, I'll take that one"

Karaoke bars. This story has very little useful information other than to help you avoid being scammed in a far off land, so I'll keep it short. It was the first weekend of me being in China and I had met up with a couple of other Australian gents I found in a market. (Turns out you can hear the Aussie accent from over one hundred meters away. Sounds like a two-stroke stuck in second gear). We asked for the taxi driver to take us to a club or a bar, at least that's what we thought we asked for. Where he took us turned out to be part of a well-planned, finely tuned machine that would see us loose hundreds of Australian dollars in a matter of minutes. It was as simple as this. We turn up to a bar, we are ushered in to a room, then made to sit on a couch. We are then presented with a food platter and beers for all. Asking what the food is for is pointless as no one speaks English. Then come the girls. No less than a dozen scantily clad Chinese girls begin dancing in front of us and singing 80s top 40. After five minutes of this rubbish we decide to move on. We stand, and begin to make our way to the door wondering where we pay, when a gentleman presents us with a bill of thousands of Yuan, which worked out to be about $500 Australian. This was broken down to all the food, beer and dancing girls. None of which we asked for, though was billed for at ten times the average Chinese price.

Some of these are solid methods, (not the karaoke bar) and only need adjustment as per situation. Keep in mind though, no matter how good the close, and how good a deal they got, they will either realize they have been closed later, and feel had, or a mate will tell them they have been when they relay the story to them.

If you have a close you want to use, make it yours and make it natural, don't even think of it as a close, rather think of it as a settlement. They the customer have come to an understanding, or agreed on a product or service, you have done a fine job on negotiating the price, and now it is time to settle, not close, settle. If people end up with what they need and want at a great price, they will be bitter at you and feel tricked by a close. But if you have been the one to provide a smooth and painless settlement, then you are the one they will keep coming back to.

Remember.

Settle

4 Don't Beat-em Join-em

The traditional way of dealing with competitors is to spend all your energy pushing them out of the market.
We would focus on offering lower prices, better service or free delivery. Essentially, more for less. Even thinking about competition will make you think competitively. Not an entirely bad thing, but it does take the focus off the customer. It changes your mind set from trying to gain something to trying to get rid of something. It's just a negative way of focusing your efforts rather than a positive focus.
So what if we flipped that around?
What if instead of trying to change the world using demolition and destruction, we changed the world using the law of attraction?
Change the way you think to a more magnetic view of the world and instead of looking for enemies to kill off, look for allies to join. Look for people to join your way of thinking and seek out like business with complementary products in the same industry that your customers deal with.

> *you will be far better off in the long run, when you realize the fact that seeking allegiance, is a better option than seeking to plunder what someone else has done the work for.*

If you sell sugar, look to align yourself with coffee manufacturers. If you sell pens, look for someone who sells pencil cases. If you offer legal consultations, join forces with a

31

financial advice firm. When you strive to set yourself up with an allied service, you begin to see things in a potential growth rather than decline.

Looking to take over a competitors business, in a way, is you admitting you cannot find the business elsewhere and have chosen to take it from someone else. If however you manage to join with another product or service, you will naturally gain all the business without all the bad karma.

There are many advantages and there are also a few disadvantages to this business model. As far as the advantages go, and this depends on the level of communication, the strongest would have to be the fact you can talk to and bounce ideas off someone in the same industry. You will be able to talk about the industry trends, new technologies and competitors. The other advantage of aligning your business is the referrals and contact lists. Referrals are by far the best new customers, for this simple reason, the credibility has come from the referee.

There are of course grey areas to alignment. Sometimes joining forces with someone is more trouble than its worth. I have seen many cases where the relationship either simply did not work or one of the two partners decided to get in the others line of work, effectively becoming a competitor. Overall though, the old way was to obliterate competition. The new way is to look for partners or people to join you.

Remember
Join.

5 We need loyal customers, not happy customers.

The old way of thinking is to strive all our customers to be happy customers. We used to believe, if someone buys something from us and they leave happy with the transaction, then all will be well and they will return again and again.

There are several places this falls down.

First of all, for some people there is just no way on earth to make them happy. We can give them a free gift, a massage on the way out, and they will complain about the massage, ask to exchange the gift for an upgrade or sell it on eBay.

Also, we seem to forget, happiness has only a small role if any in the many reasons people buy things. If we go to the supermarket we are shopping out of necessity, and with the self-service checkout we don't even get a happy smile. If we are shopping for gifts we could be shopping out of obligation, or with kids, the experience may be anything but happy.

> *Sometimes price service and quality have very little to do with repeat custom.*

Finally, if we are a reseller, we are shopping with our customers in mind, considering if they will buy what we are thinking is a good thing. In other words the emotion is typically removed from the equation.

33

We don't need happy customers, we need loyal customers. We need satisfied, loyal customers. If you think back to all the times you returned to a store, you will realize you rarely ever went beck because you had a happy or elated shopping experience. You returned because they either marketed something well enough to entice you, you needed something and knew they had it, or it may have even been just plain convenient to go there. Sometimes price service and quality have very little to do with repeat custom. Have a look at a busy food court and tell me where the queue is, McDonalds. A food court has a plethora (I love that word) of foods from any number of places around the world. Choice, value and quality. But they still queue at McDonalds. McDs' have a loyal following. The customers may not even know they are loyal to the fast food chain. Because it begins at such an early age, most McHumans believe it is just the way things are meant to be. It's not good for you, most of us can make a better burger at home, yet they are consistently on top of the food chain. They have loyalty, they have market share, and they have satisfied customers consistently around the world. Micky Ds understand what they need to do to keep people coming back. Reasonably priced food, consistent quality, catering for a wide range of demographics.

What do you need to do?

There are many things you can do that will get your customers to return to you, time and time again. Loyalty cards work well for starters, with this added little tip. If you plan on say having a free car wash for every five paid washes, get a card with seven notches on it and punch out the first two. Of for free coffee after every sixth cup, get a card with eight little cups on it and punch out the first two for them. They will think you are doing them a huge favor and believe they are already well on their way to a freebie.

Get in to a twelve month marketing campaign with a sole plan to build loyalty. Free collectable gifts, happy endings, long running competitions, family days, and rewards for referrals. Focus only on building loyalty for at least once a week. Have a loyalty focused sales meeting.

Amongst all the other things like, value, service and satisfaction. The focus on loyalty needs to be in your top five.

What will get people to return to you time and time again?

Loyalty doesn't mean customers prefer to deal with you or even that you are doing a better job than the competition, you should be, but it doesn't mean that. Loyalty is just that. People are loyal to you, they return to you time and time again for any number of reasons. Regular training sessions, information days, form a club, form a religion (it worked for L. Ronald Hubbard). Anything you can think of to get them through your door again.

Newsagents will have magazines with little components to a battle ship or aircraft, every month they release another magazine with a component. It's a fantastic idea because it creates an unbreakable loyalty and typically you will learn the history as you build the model.

Every printer you buy has a different cartridge, sure they could make it to fit the previous model, but they are creating a loyalty to the manufacturer, at least until the aftermarket manufacturers catch up.

The same goes for mobile phones chargers, car components and investment companies.

Investment companies?

Have you ever been to an investment seminar of sorts, something on real-estate, or share trading?

They only ever give you a small portion of the information to get you interested, especially if it is a free seminar. They may advertise it as a "learn how to trade the stock market", and at the end of the seminar, all you have learnt is how they are going to show you a few more things, if you cough up some cash that is. Basically it's the same as the model magazine, only with information. Like the seminar the first magazine is very cheap if not free, then like the investment company information, the price goes up as you require more and more.

This isn't scamming or a trick of any kind, for the most part these people have worked hard to produce what you have been offered. They have simply found a way to break down the payments and keep you on board. Some people may not be able to afford a one off fee anyway.

If you can break down a part of your business and sell it as components, you are well on your way to building a loyal following. Not like, one shoe for five dollars and the second for fifty, rather, I'll show you how to walk for ten dollars a week, and at the end you get a free pair of shoes.

Change your focus to getting loyalty.

Remember

Loyalty

6   Transfer this!

The old school sales teachers will tell you that a sale takes place when there is a transfer of enthusiasm.

The theory was that if you get excited enough about something, that excitement will pass on to other people in the same room. We were told to get fired up at presentations and the excitement will be contagious. I never really liked the word contagious. It makes me think of sickness and disease being passed on to otherwise healthy people. This belief to get all fired up about things is still strong in the network marketing business and a necessary commodity when selling devices that slice and dice fruit and vegetables' like never before, at two in the morning.

If we are to get excited in a sales presentation, either consulting or demonstrating to a customer or prospect, one of two things will happen.

A, they will think we are on drugs or mentally disturbed.

Or

B, they will think we are trying way too hard to get the message across, thus instilling doubt that the product will stand on its own two feet.

It is also a little insulting to intelligent people who will see right through the fist-pumping performance.

There is of course a level of enthusiasm required to show you have faith in what you are selling. As you would tell a friend about a good restaurant or bar, you display a genuine commitment, and strength in your belief. And this is what is transferred today, a belief.

"This is the best I have seen" not "this is the most amazing awesome thing ever".

It's like this. Enthusiasm comes after belief. You must first discover a belief and have faith in a product or service to get enthusiastic about it. Otherwise it is a lie.

Try and get enthusiastic about something you don't believe in. You can't, yet you can believe in something you aren't enthusiastic about. I believe a particular brand of car tyre is the best. I do not get enthusiastic about it for the simple reason I have no strong argument for it other than it felt safe in the wet and lasted a long time. This is the same for many chosen products for myself, and I'll bet you have yours too. Like a shampoo, deodorant, brand of pasta sauce or make of car. You have your beliefs without having a crazy enthusiasm towards them. We were told it was good so we tried it and liked it. Now we use and believe in it. If we tell a friend about it, they may try it even if we simply say "it's a good thing", because they **trust** us.

> *As you would tell a friend about a good restaurant or bar, you display a genuine commitment, and strength in your belief. And this is what is transferred today, a belief.*

So that trust thing must be the start of all this again, we keep coming back to it. If they trust you, you almost don't need any enthusiasm; they will believe you, period.

Think of the level of enthusiasm you may have when you would tell family and friends about a great movie, and that is your only

required level of enthusiasm. Anything above that will just look too much like an infomercial, and they will sit looking at you with one eyebrow cocked, patiently waiting for you to finish, then upload the video of you bouncing around to YouTube's funniest salesmen channel.
A simple "you're going to love this" may be enough to get the level there.
Keep it natural and they will believe you. The transfer of belief is what we are going for.
Five hundred years ago we believed the sun and the moon both passed around the earth, and that we were the center of the solar system. All our senses tell us this is the most likely situation. We can see every day, both the moon and the sun rise, pass over the sky, and set on the other side. None of us have ever seen the earth move. We have seen footage of it moving, but we have never seen it move.

In the 16th century a new idea was proposed by the Polish astronomer Nicolai Copernicus, that the sun was at the center of our solar system and all other planets orbited the sun. He called this The Heliocentric System.

Now, we all have an unshakable belief that the sun is indeed at the center of our solar system.
Why? How have we been sold on something that goes against our very own senses?
Well it's not enthusiasm.
The reason we believe this to be true is because we were all taught the physics and shown how they are applied to the moon and the sun by people we trust. Education, plus insight and trust.
No amount of enthusiasm would ever change a person's beliefs. Not without trust anyway. Imagine what Copernicus went through when he first presented his findings. He would have gathered his data spoke with authority and provided insight thus gaining trust, then and only then would he have had their belief.

If we try and transfer enthusiasm, without first listening, educating and advising, then all we are going to have is an enthusiastic person, and that enthusiasm will evaporate over a short period of time, or worse.

Say we have an idiot. If we are enthusiastic around an idiot without first trying to inform and advise them, then all we are going to have is an enthusiastic idiot.

Don't start with enthusiasm; rather start with advice and insight with the intention of creating a solid belief.

Remember
Belief

7 Experience is useless

Well, it's not completely useless. It can be handy if you are a tradesman, a doctor or a fireman. But if you're looking to be a sales professional, experience can not only be useless, it can be a burden, or even detrimental.

You know how the jobs market will advertise for someone with experience. All other qualifications are usually secondary, well they have it all wrong, especially in sales positions. What they really need to be asking for is someone with good values and a solid set of principles.

Any martial arts teacher will tell you, it is easier to teach someone who has never learned martial arts before. To teach someone who has experience in another discipline requires the un-learning of that set of skills that years of training have developed all the habits and reflexes in to an automatic response. The experience within is ingrained and habitual. It becomes a part of who you are so much so, you need not think about your actions. This philosophy of a punch sums it up.

> *Knowledge gives you confidence. Experience makes you think you have knowledge*

A punch is first just a punch, then it is more than a punch, then it becomes just a punch.

This can be related to any learnt skill. It begins as a move, motion or act, then becomes more complicated and technical, then becomes a natural part of you.

Do you think this is a good idea in the ever changing world of sales?

What we are teaching our children in school will be obsolete by the time they need to use it. What we learn in sales today will not be relevant tomorrow, though we will have the experience so engrained in us we will fail to see there are better ways. Just as we wear clothes fitting our generation and say that's the way we have always done it, so too will we tell our customers "we have a hot deal on the line for today only would they like the red or the blue!"

Experience in sales will show us one thing and one thing only, what has worked in the past, and that is precisely what we need to examine in detail.

But doesn't experience give you confidence?

No, knowledge gives you confidence. Experience makes you think you have knowledge, and by the way, by the time you have the necessary experience to be confident you are never going to catch up to the ones who learned what they needed to be great in sales.

So what is needed to know, if experience is not the answer?

What have all the job adverts and recruitment agencies got wrong?

And if not experience then what should we be seeking to learn?

Principles

Only principles will stand the test of time.

What is useful today will be obsolete tomorrow, so anything to do with experience alone will be rendered useless.

You need not have years of experience to excel in the selling world. Forget studying sales one liners, opens and closes. Learn principles and you will be set for the rest of your career as the world moves forward.

Now the old school will tell you to practice pitches and scripts, to reword them and make them yours. With all sorts of if/then responses to their questions.

Principles are the only thing that will not change with fashion, and they will not need a review.

Principles will not become corny or outdated and we can teach them to any who will learn them as fast as they like.

> *If you are well fed and you have a warm, safe bed then you are luckier than more than half the people on the planet.*

Og mandinos book The Greatest Salesman in the World uses a set of scrolls told in a story to describe the necessary lessons required to be a great sales person. The first scroll tells us what he thinks about experience.

Now I wouldst become the greatest of olive trees and, in truth, the greatest of salesmen. And how will this be accomplished? For I have neither the knowledge nor the experience to achieve greatness and already I have stumbled in ignorance and fallen into pools of self-pity. The answer is simple. I will commence my journey unencumbered with either the weight of unnecessary knowledge or the handicap of meaningless experience. Nature already has supplied me with knowledge and instinct far greater than any beast in the forest and the value of <u>experience is overrated, usually by old men who nod wisely and speak stupidly.</u>

Og Mandino, The Greatest Salesman In the World.

A small part of one chapter of a brilliant book. I highly recommend it.

The rest of that chapter describes the first principle which is to form good habits. Good habits are the key to success, bad habits will ensure failure. It takes twenty one days to make or break any habit, so get to it.

A good habit is merely self-discipline rehearsed to a point where it becomes a natural part of you, and so turning you in to a better person. This is not a book on discipline, so I will close this chapter with this. The single most important principle you need to develop is self-disciple. Without it, nothing you ever study in any book or classroom will ever have an effect on your life other than the wasted time and money.

Discipline is doing what you need to do, when you need to do it, whether you feel like it or not.

Practice self-discipline and you will prosper in any chosen field. I could write an entire set of books on this one topic, indeed others have, but I'll just say start with self-discipline in every aspect of your life and watch as every aspect of your life flourishes.

There are only two other principles you cannot deviate from and they are.

1, Live honestly.

     Always tell the truth to others and to yourself regardless of the consequences that may follow as a result.

2, Be grateful.

     If you are well fed and you have a warm, safe bed then you are luckier than more than half the people on the planet. Be grateful for your children are not being taken in to child soldier camps. Be grateful you have the ability to read this book and for anything else you may have previously taken for granted, and for the fact you can choose to be a salesperson.

All other principles need to come from you, yes from you. Surprised! Well you shouldn't be, it is your life after all. I'm not about to tell you what kind of person you are.
They can be ones like
Live in the moment
Laugh at life

or Learn to forgive.

You need to be the one to come up with your own set of life principles. In fact I suggest you allow five minutes now to do this before you get stuck in to the next chapter. Go on, this will be (your name)'s life principles. Put it on the fridge, change or add to it at will and prepare to discover the true values in life worth fighting for.

Remember
Principles'

8 Don't follow up to get a sale

WHAT!!

That's right. Don't follow up to get the sale.

Of course you always want to follow up after the sale, but if you have done your job in the presentation of your product or service, the customer will have all the information they need to make a decision.
The follow up is for chumps who can't get a customer to say yes or no.

Historically we would show someone a product or service, and they would say, "oh gee gosh can I think about it?" and you might say something like "sure thing you great customer you. I'll get back to you in a week and we can talk then".

NO!

We finish the meeting there and then.
I will go in to dealing with an objection a little more later on in the book, but for now just understand this one thing. You have a meeting, and that is the meeting to discuss the sale. When you understand this you will begin to find ways of dealing with the no's and objections there and then, instead of the easy way out of a follow up.

"Hey I work hard, I'm not looking for the easy way"

Sure you do, what I mean by easy way is the one that takes a little more effort to understand how to deal with the procrastinators of the world.

Brian Tracy says, when a customer tells him they will get back to him he says politely " you know everything you need to know, in fact in a few days you will have forgotten most of what I have just told you so why not just decide now because then we can move on." Use the word *because* whenever you need to explain something. "Because" is the great justifier in a sentence.

In my role as a traveling salesman, I would travel from factory to farm showing off the very best in hardware nuts' and bolts', lubricants and workshop equipment. My main focus would be the days, weeks, and month's budget. I fast came to the understanding I had a limited window of selling time, that the greatest selling hours of the day where between 9am and 11am, the rest of the day, the success rate trickles off. So given this limited window of opportunity, it wasn't long before I began looking for the best way to get the gold in that short time frame.

> *A re-schedule is not a follow up, it is what we do with a consultant. Salesmen follow-up. Another meeting means we start again at a new level a different level.*

What is the fastest way to get a sale? The answer is, to GET the sale. I was never really good at following up anyway. It seemed no matter how many notes I took and how well I planned, I used to end up showing the same thing again using the same strategies and the same closes. Hearing the same thing again made me look like an infomercial and thus be more of a deterrent to the sale. I got to the point of using old school follow-up talk

"I was calling to follow up on the proposal."

"I am calling to see if you had any questions.'

"I just wanted to make sure you got my e-mail."

"The reason for my follow up was to see if you had come to a decision."

If you are in an industry that requires a follow up situation, like real-estate or car sales where people are going to make a big decision. No matter how good you are at closing, sometimes people just need time to decide and all you are going to do is piss them off by trying to close. In this instance we still do not follow up.

Let's say you sell million dollar apartments. The customer typically needs time to work out the details. That's great, but you still **don't do a follow up**! You find out the issues they have and book another meeting. After a product or service presentation of any kind you should have one of three results,

Yes,

No,

Or a scheduled meeting.

A re-schedule is not a follow up, it is what we do with a consultant. Salesmen follow-up. Another meeting means we start again at a new level a different level. We go through the process again. Remember they will most likely have forgotten the vast majority of your information, even if it's the very next day, more than half of what you have told them will not have been accurately retained.

To get another meeting, we could simply say something like, "need some time to think it over? Sure, let's go over this on Thursday and I'll get those answers on the colour and extras for you before then". You need to have a reason to get back to them other than getting a yes or no answer. We need to above all make them feel comfortable from the start, like we are going on a date with the intention of getting them in the sack, and remember, they are the ones taking the risk with this sale, not you, so appreciate their hesitation, I'll get in to that one later too.

For now though let me take a step back for a moment. Following up can be, and I say **can be**, very one eyed, or narrow minded. You need to know what it's like to have a feeling of being under that much pressure. What may be a small decision for you may be a massive decision to them, so show the same care and understanding for all of your sales. To help you understand a little better, I have a little game for you. It's called the tapping game. The tapping game needs two or more people with a similar knowledge base of music. Pick a song you know the other person will know, and without telling the other person what it is, begin to tap out the song on the table. Just tap, tap, tap, the tune and then ask them to guess the song you are tapping. Here's the thing, they never ever get the song. It will drive you nuts because you know the song so well in your own head, and the tune is so clear to you, it's hard for you to understand why they cannot pick it. If you have someone nearby try it now, but be warned, you will find yourself saying "oh, c'mon, it's easy". Now switch sides, and become the listener. Going through this tapping game process will help you understand what it's like to hold all the cards, and also be the one to hold none of them.

Why is gaining such a deep understanding so important? Because without this understanding, you will continue to search for a decision without ever attempting to understand what made them hesitate in the first place. When we get a no, or a maybe we must understand this is a call for help, a call out for more information.

A follow up, we shall now refer to as a second meeting. A second meeting is for people who feel a decision on the spot is just too much of a big decision on the day and they need time. Remember the tapping game at this point, and what they must be going through. If and when you do

> *When we get a no, or a maybe we must understand this is a call for help.*

make a time for a second meeting, remember this. You are not meeting to get the sale. You are meeting to close the sale as if it was the end of the presentation on day one and you just stepped outside for a moment, to get an answer on the colour, and changed clothes, and got a haircut, and came back a week later you get my drift.

I'll say it one more time. Do not do a Follow-Up to get the sale! If you really need to meet later, have something they need you to get back to them about and make it another meeting or a meet-up. Go over the facts and answer the issues they had last meeting. You will be better received for it.

Think of it this way, old school salesmen follow up, but friends, lovers and consultants meet-up.

We are striving to be different and looking to be the consultant. If you are still not convinced and you are sure your follow ups are going just fine, answer me this, out loud, I'm listening. What do you tell people when you are making a follow up appointment?

Do you tell them you are scheduling a follow up?

If not, then stop calling it a follow up to yourself, because you are already booking second meetings' like a consultant and ten points to you. If yes, then try the second meeting idea or forever hold your peace. If you don't book at all, but rather do a follow up phone call, then you need to start booking appointments face to face. If you cannot visit them and you must call them, then have at least one piece of additional information for them. Also go over some of the main points. A refresher if you will.

This is going to be a tough one for some sales professionals to get in to the swing of. We need to remember we are there for the customer to be the best consultant and adviser they will think of when they are looking to purchase. If we shift the process in to a follow up situation, we will begin to turn what is an advisory and insightful meeting in to a sales presentation and a close, which is precisely what I am trying to say we need to step away from. Not a follow up, just a second half to what is that same game.

Don't follow-up to close a sale. Re-schedule, meet-up, or re-visit and reinforce their trust in you.

Remember

Meet-up

9 Don't ask for the sale more than once

The old way of thinking, was to ask at least five times for the sale during a presentation. I'm not suggesting this is an entirely bad idea just that asking someone for the same thing more than once can be a little insulting to their intelligence, and in this day and age, the vast majority of your customers will be wise to the repeated request tactic. I once went to a seminar where the guy presenting was well in to the repeated request routine. The first twenty minutes was him giving us all the information we actually needed, then for the next half an hour, he simply repeated what he had already told us, while he was continually asking for a sale "wouldn't you agree", "can you see the benefit" and "does this sound like something you would use". By asking someone the same question over and over we are either going to wear them down to a yes, or turn them off completely, neither is a good sales result. Think of a child asking for a toy in a supermarket.

"Can I have it?"
"No"
"Please"
"No"
"But I want it"
And again and again until either
"NO" or "FINE, HAVE IT!"

Never ask for the sale more than once, unless, you give them another reason to change their mind.

This is the only reason we should go on and ask for the sale again. We have provided them with additional information and they are now a little savvier to what we are selling them. Without the additional information, we are asking them to forget their last decision and mind set, and have another go. We need to give people a reason to re-consider their decision and why.

My eight year old daughter has the negotiation down-pat
"Can I have it?"
"No"
"I'll give you a kiss"
I then might request a cuddle as well, and the deal is done.

Never ask for the sale more than once, unless you show the customer or prospect either a better option, or an extra. Listen to the reason they said no and work with it. You are a consultant! Ask them why they think it is not for them. You need to work with people and show them all the reasons they need to make the best decision for them, not for you. If they are sitting there listening to you, then they must have an interest in what you have. It's up to you to find out what it is.

> *Never ask for the sale more than once, unless you show the customer or prospect either a better option, or an extra.*

If, on the other hand, you ask them if they like the idea, product or service and they say yes, assume it is a yes for the sale and move on to the next item, or ask for payment. To assume the sale is not a bad way to go. For the most part they will just go with it letting you drive the ship, and at worst they will pull you up, at which point you apologize and ask what the issue is. Ask for the sale and be done with it.

Asking for a sale once and getting a no is actually a good thing. It allows you to refine, and find out why, and what you can do to get the yes you need. This means you will have a better suited product for your customer.

Seller "Do you want to buy this?"
Buyer "No"
Seller "What are your concerns?"
Buyer "Uhh, I just don't think we need it right now"
Seller "You don't need it now?" (This is a reflective question. Just bouncing back what they just said to get them to think about the answer they just gave. Doctors do it all the time. "The pain is in your head you say" patient "well it's more at the top of my spine".)
Buyer "well we do need it, but we don't have the funding"
Seller "If we can make it an extra month to pay, or work out some terms, will that help?"
Buyer "Well yes, I guess it will"
Seller "ok, I'll draw it up for three months"

Ask for the sale once. If you get a no, deal with it by asking 'why' at least three times to get to the real reason, and then offer a solution.

Ask once, then listen.

Remember

Once

10 Fear the Reaper

Venditophobia

The fear of salespeople.

Actually I just made that up. Hope it sticks though. Venditor, is Latin for salesman meaning seller, or vendor. Nothing for saleswoman, sorry ladies.

Surprisingly there is no actual term for the fear of sales people. We have Scatophobia: Fear of fecal matter, Hagiophobia: Fear of saints or holy things, and Philosophobia: Fear of philosophy. The funny (as in funny strange) thing is there are enough people out there with a fear of Philosophy to give it a title, yet there are many more with a fear of sales people, I know of some. I can't say I know anyone with a deep fear of fecal matter though.

So why do you think people fear a salesperson?
Some people hate them, and some don't much care for them but some people really fear sitting at a meeting table opposite a man in a suit with something to sell. It's as if the salesman is working on a well-crafted plan to rob them of everything they own, Reap them. See the movie *Matchstick Men* for an idea of what can be done to an unsuspecting person.
Let's look at fear. The definition of fear is described as,
an unpleasant emotion caused by the threat of danger, pain, or harm.

This can be translated to financial pain and harm. People will fear making a buying mistake for the potential harm it will cause them. This may not have come about as a result of a past experience, most fears aren't, though all fears have been learnt. And so they can also be unlearnt, even phobias.

> *Some people really fear sitting at a meeting table opposite a man in a suit with something to sell.*

So if there are some out there who fear the salesperson, (this may manifest in anger, dismissal, or even aggression) how can we look to move past it? What can we do as professionals, to show them we are wanting to help them, and not hurt them?

First we need to understand, this may have been developed over years, decades, or even generations. I know my two little girls have battled with a fear of spiders in their younger years, a fear passed on from their loving mother. Every time a customer has been burnt by a salesman with all the sales tactics and tricks we have come to know and love, they have added to an ever increasing shell or wall. They may have had a family member or a close friend loose a large sum of money in a real-estate investment and have decided to blame the agent, thus falsely creating a fear. However it came about, if they think you are trying to break down that wall you will only instill and build a defensive fear wall, either in the form of more aggression, shyness or just a slammed door. The only way to overcome this is with the two fear weapons of credibility and trust.

Like I say at the beginning of this book, focus on building trust and the rest will fall in to place. The fear of making a buying mistake fades away the more trust we have. We can start building trust with credibility, and the best way to build credibility to overcome fear, is product and business knowledge. I'll get in to this more later on in the book. Stories of success in the same type of business will be a great place to start as well. It's important to use true stories, though they need not be yours.

Let's walk a mile in their shoes. Imagine taking a large portion of your savings account or getting out a loan that would make you consider living on rice for the first five years of the term. Taking that money and putting it all on red at the roulette table. Feel your heart beat through your chest. Palms sweaty, blood runs cold, sphincter tightening. This is the fight or flight response, and when a customer is faced with the big financial decision we are putting to them, this is what they may be going through. The part of the brain called the amygdala is triggered whenever a stressful situation is presented, the amygdala then sends a rapid-fire of signals to areas of the brain and body. The adrenal glands release stress hormones called cortisol. Fats and sugar is released from your liver in to the blood stream. Lungs increase in breathing rate to get more oxygen to the heart. The whole cardio vascular system increases its operation to ensure more supply to the muscles. The digestive system shuts down and the senses heighten. All the while, your brain begins to switch off and release chemicals to unneeded areas like the frontal cortex. The area responsible for speech decision making and rationale so as to focus the needed areas, like impulse control. Ask any self-respecting woman what she would go through on the first sexual encounter with a new partner and she will tell you this is the feeling she has. It's dammed scary. Imagine, this is what some of your customers go through when making a purchasing decision, and it doesn't need to be a big decision. Some people will fear choosing a set of curtains or an interior color scheme. Imagine a house, or a game changing business decision. Empathize with them, don't sympathize with them. Empathize.

Sympathize is saying "oh I know, I had the same choice to make last year and I did… I went to… and I… I … I" they don't care about you, this is their moment. Empathy is saying something like "This is a mighty big choice here, let's make it really easy to back out at any time here, any time, and you get all your hard earned money back". Or if you can't give them the money back "I understand this is a mighty big choice here, and I'm going to make it really easy to back out at any time here, I want you to be 100%

on this so if you're a little concerned, take a walk and meet back here in ten" or before we sign off on this, let's get a hot chocolate". Side note, the funny thing about hot chocolate is it is an extremely comforting drink, most everyone likes it and it has no caffeine to get people anxious.

Basically we just need to convey the fact we understand what they are feeling, and reiterate to them they have an out if they want it. The second they feel backed in to a corner, show them there is a door behind them if they need it.

Knowing your customer may be having this feeling of fear, wouldn't you want to help them through this process, and not let them even come close to feeling it in the first place?

This fear is real and it is crippling. Know it is there and be professional about it. If it's not love holding them back its fear, so show them you know what you are talking about, offer them a way out, give them time and a cuppa coco.

Remember

Empathize

11 What are we fighting for?

As a sales person, have you ever got up on a Monday morning and said to yourself, 'what on earth am I doing in sales? What's the point of sales people anyway?

Not so long ago, the world needed sales men and women to visit them, educate them, show them new products or services and handle complaints. Now, everything I just mentioned can be acquired online, well, so the customers are led to believe anyway. Your customers now think they can look anything up and not have a representative call on them to push what they don't need, or potentially waste their time.

If people want something, they will just go online and buy it. All I'm doing as a salesperson is adding to the cost of the item. Am I needed? Do they want me? What am I doing driving for hours if they can just email me? What's it all for?

Of course *you* have felt that way before haven't you? It is a tough job, and at times it can be extremely thankless.

Why do we do what we do?

Why do we sell?

What is *your* true motivator?

> *Is money distracting you from being great at your job?*

Now I'm going to assume something here, and I know, to assume is to make an ass of you and me (ass-u-me), but I'll give it a go any ways.

I'll assume you enjoy the physical job description of selling. What I mean by job description is, getting dressed up, brushing your hair, putting on a nice pair of shoes and shaking hands with customers, the basic action of being a sales person. In other words, let's say your superior called you in the morning and said "hello my beloved employee, we can't pay you for today's work, but please continue as if nothing had changed". Or if you work for yourself, you got a letter from the tax office saying "hello my beloved tax payer, kindly pay us your days earnings for this day whatever it may be" Would you do a normal day's work looking after your customers, or would you stay at home drinking coffee or tea, watching TV and burning ants with a magnifying glass. If you said you would stay at home, I'm afraid you may want to consider a career change. You may be in it for the money and money alone. However if I have assumed correct, (is that correct or correctly?) then you enjoy what you do, you would continue to work for a day without pay, rather to look after your customers. You may even answer your phone on the weekend now, knowing full well you are not getting paid for it. If this is the case, and you enjoy your work, we can continue. This is important, we need to be sure of this now, because no one ever made a fortune doing something they didn't love. All the greats, Jobs, Gates, Zuckerberg, Branson, Trump, the list goes on. They all loved or still love what they do.

If you enjoy your work enough to say "ok, I'm not getting money today but I'll still do my job" then we have good foundation for you to make a fortune.

First, we need to check your focus.

The old school focus used to be money and money alone. Focusing on things like toys and commissions. We would focus on making target to get the bonus or make the promotion for a better income. I once had a boss offer me $50 if I could open three accounts in the one day, I told him to keep his money and I'll just take the challenge thanks. This caught him off guard. He thought he offended me and started to apologize until I said to him, "Brad", I mean "Mr. Smith, you can keep your money because I have more noble motivators, and the money distracts me from my focus". Come to think of it I think I told him to make it interesting and he offered me more money! Or something like that. You get what I'm saying though, my point is, don't work just for the money. Money will come regardless, as a byproduct of what you're doing well.

Financial reward narrows focus and dulls creativity.
Daniel H Pink

In Daniel Pink's book Drive, he talks about how when we do a job for money, we lose our desire to do the job. Working for money is a very short term way of getting what you want, and it will never be enough.

Is money distracting you from being great at your job?

When you focus on the wrong thing, that being just the money and/or targets rather than getting the right thing to the right person, you get to a point where you will do whatever you can to get the sale.

We are looking for a chemical hit called oxytocin. This is the bonding drug the brain releases. It's the 'help someone feel good drug'.

Ever sold something to someone, who deep down you knew didn't need it, or worse, couldn't afford it? Felt pretty lousy didn't you.

If you are a good person, which in our cores I believe we all are, you probably felt like you stole something.

Provided you have a reasonably good moral compass, selling something to someone who does not have the need for it, nor the means to pay for what you have just skillfully (I use that term loosely) convinced them to buy, should have made you feel like you committed an offence against your inner humanity. On the other hand, if you have sold something of value to a person who needs it, this should make you feel good inside.

Have you ever said or heard someone say

"I just like selling, dunno why, but I just do".

This is because deep down we are helping someone, and in turn we are getting helped back. Sure the money, commissions, or area growth may be the initial goal and the reason you initiated the meeting or applied for the job in the first place, but that good feeling you get when you know a sale has gone through on a win-win, and the customer is grateful for all your work, is an addictive feeling.

In fact it is the same feeling fire fighters, rescue workers and those in the medical trade get when they help someone in need. The feeling is so good many people in these industries are volunteers. I know pulling someone from a car wreck isn't the same as selling a pair of shoes, but the brain doesn't know that, and so the reaction in the brain is the same.

We are looking for a chemical hit called oxytocin. This is the bonding drug the brain releases. It's the 'help someone feel good drug'.

We get it from feeding puppies and helping an old person cross the road. We get it from tying a child's shoe laces and saving whales. We get so used to this oxytocin hit, that we have subconsciously identified its feeling and what we can do to get it. So we go in search of it.

Not sure about what I'm saying? Try this for self-test.

Go out and do a random act of kindness. It's important that no money is involved. Something like, sitting with an old person at a nursing home, reading a story to a sick child in hospital, offer your seat to someone in need, or letting someone in front in a line. The best one I had recently was a friend offering to babysit when they were in town because they thought we may enjoy a night out.

Do one of these things and take note of the feeling you get. For a true control test, go out and say something mean to an innocent dog (they can take it, English is usually not their first language). The funny thing is even though you know they can't understand you, it makes you feel bad.

Then go out and offer a gold coin for someone's shopping trolley, or clean the dishes off a street café table. Even if no one notices it, you feel great.

Acknowledge that feeling in your heart and take some time to feel it.

Now you know this little gem, make yourself aware of the feeling you get when you have a good sale, leaving you and the customer happy. It should be a sale you had a big part in making happen, not a retail sale that would have happened regardless but a contact and close sale, a hand shake and a thank you letter. When the warm and fuzzies have well and truly set in, go out and smile at people, and watch as they smile back, and build you up even higher until you have another sale on the books and look forward to the good stuff that is oxytocin, surging through your body on a mission to making you feel great.

That, is why we do what we do.

We know it is good and our body lets us feel it is good, so if we do it enough to recognize the feeling as good then we will do it more, even to the point of habit, a good habit. That is the only difference between a helpful person and a passerby, the good habit they have come to own.

Have you ever seen video footage of someone falling off the platform on to the train tracks, and there seems to ever only be one or two people jump down and help them. Or seen an elderly person struggling to get over the crossing until someone gets out of their car and helps them, leaving all the other drivers sitting there wondering how long this is going to take.

These good people have developed such good habits in helping others they subconsciously look for situations where they can help. Without knowing it they are looking for that hit of oxytocin.

That is who we as sales professionals can become. Seek to help and look after people and they will be forever building you up to be a naturally good person. Look for a situation where you can help, look for opportunities where you can build a good feeling habit and observe yourself as you change in to a better person, before your very eyes.

Try this little experiment and you will see. Just for five days, just five, search for any and all helping things you can do. Look for the ones who need you. Feed a horse a carrot if you are struggling. Seek and you will find many where help is needed. Ask a rotary club or a school. Here's an idea make a customer's day. Deliver their goods personally saving them the freight. Offer them a free voucher for your service, get them a coffee.

Do some good and acknowledge the feeling.

Look for that feeling in your everyday work.

This is why you sell.

This is why you do what you do.

Remember

Feeling

12 What's the problem

In the good old days, we would gather as much information as we possibly could and bombard the customer with it. Have you ever used the phrase *features benefits and advantages*? Guess what, they already know the features, quite possibly better than you do. And there is little or no advantage if the customer believes they already have it covered, so they will never see the benefit if you fail to find out what they really need.

The old method is to offer to make things better for the customer. Build a better mouse trap and the world will beat a path to your door they used to say, but if they don't think they have a problem then they won't see the solution no matter how good a mouse trap you have. You may very well be able to build a fully automated mouse trap that will hunt out and humanly execute every mouse within a ten kilometer radius, but if they want to fight a termite infestation, you will struggle to sell them. They may have a mouse problem and not even know it. If you discover this and bring it to their attention, then you will be the exterminator they will turn to. We first need to find the real problem, and tell the customer what it is.

The old way is to provide information, information, and then more information. Now, our customers can get that anywhere. Everywhere they look they can find comparisons, examples and even product instructional videos. Information is so plentiful, it becomes less valuable. You are in effect giving a customer what they can get for themselves. Granted it is more refined and possibly a little more relevant, depending on your ability to filter, regardless, information is now as common as dirt.

This is where you come in. Although there may be all the information they need, it might just take them a life time to find the needle they are looking for in the mountain of hay stacks, and if they do find it, are they going to know what to do with it.

This is especially true in the legal and medical industry where a new term for people who research and diagnose their own illness has been coined.

Catherine was worried. For weeks she had been experiencing nervous twitching in muscles all over her body. So, she did what millions of us would do, she Googled the phrase 'muscle twitching'. If you were to do the search yourself, you would see why Catherine's concerns quickly turned to terror. Among the google results is a page on a university website about Creutzfeldt-Jakob disease (CJD), the incurable and fatal brain disease (which lists muscle twitching as a symptom), and a site about amyotrophic lateral sclerosis (ALS), another rare and fatal brain condition, also known as Lou Gehrig's disease.

> *The old way is to provide information, information, and then more information. Now, our customers can get that anywhere.*

So then panicked and irrational, Catherine then decided to see her doctor. But just as quickly as she beat a path to his door, he ruled out anything serious – after all, the chances of contracting CJD or ALS are vanishingly small. Instead, he diagnosed benign fasciculation syndrome (BFS), a medical name for a number of non-threatening symptoms that include twitching. But that wasn't enough for Catherine, who Googled "BFS" when the shakes got worse. She ended up on a forum at the site AboutBFS.com.

"New member ... terrified ... mouth and speech problems. PLEASE help", she posted. "I have been living life as if I was going to die in 18 months ... I feel like everyone thinks I'm crazy." But Catherine is no crazier than she is terminally ill. She is, however, a 'cyberchondriac', the term that describes a growing number of otherwise rational internet users who, when they present their symptoms to 'Dr Google', latch on to the worst diagnosis thrown back at them.

Catherine's story is not unique to medicine. This can and does happen in most every industry, for the simple reason that there is a mass of information without a logic filter. People will receive just enough info to make them dangerous.

More information is not what they need anymore. The new way is to offer what they will not be able to find out so easily, your wisdom and insight.

If they are not on the right path to begin with, they will waste hours and even days and dollars researching what they may not need at all, or like Catherine, the results may be even worse. With your help they may just be able to find out what it is they have been looking for, or that they ought to start looking for something in particular.

We need to take a step back and do a little figuring out to see what the problem is, and yes there will be problems there are always problems. Everything on the planet has problems, except for the dead.

Brian Tracey says we need to ask twenty times to find the real problem. Most children will need at least three rounds of questioning to get to the real issue.

Once we can clearly identify a problem, we can then go on to offer them what they really need.

There are only two kinds of people in the world, people who admit they have problems and liars. Ask them what is wrong, and then what is wrong with that and then why that is a bad thing. We need

67

to get to the bottom of their problems so we can offer a realistic insight as a solution, and if you have done your due diligence in their industry, you will know the questions to ask. If you were to go to someone who can offer insight to your own problems, you will feel they will have a much better chance of fixing them. The same is true for you and your customers, show a customer the problem and they will entrust you with the solution. Hey they may even be content with the issues you have kindly pointed out to them. My hair is turning grey, I don't care.

If and when you do find the customer's issues, use your insight and a correct line of questioning to either fix the problem or identify one they never knew they had. Then get ready for the feel good oxytocin to flow as you become a problem solver and a helper, not just a salesperson.

Remember

Problem

13 Are you unique?

The old way was to sell something by telling your customers everyone's doing it, or everyone has one. In the past this worked because we all wanted what the other guy had. We wanted to live in the same street and drive that car everyone's talking about. We didn't want to be different because that wasn't the nuclear family image. We used to want in to the herd, to give us a sense of belonging.

Now, we live in a time of abundance when we can all have a TV, a car and a mobile phone. We need a sense of uniqueness. It's not enough to say everyone's doing it, in fact this may be a put off for some, enough to make them say

> *If you think there is nothing unique about what you do, think about doughnuts.*

"no thanks, I'd rather be the point of difference". If everyone's selling the same thing then it comes down to a price war if you sell to a reseller. Or if you sell to an end user, why would the customer go to you when they can get the same thing or service next door.

Now this is not the same as providing proof by using others as an example, you should always use but a few case studies to get confidence in your product or service. What I'm referring to here is showing the customer they will be unique, and sought after. They will be special in the market place. This is not for everyone, and please understand this has always been in the background as an option. The only thing that has really changed is the percentages. There used to be but a few customers who were willing to be different, and in the past they may have been thought of as hippies, left wing and radicals. Now the tables have turned and the ones who want to be the same are the ones being left behind. The funny thing is, it doesn't even have to really be different, just so long as everyone believes it is.

Several years ago a Krispy Creams opened up near us. It was the first one in Victoria, and on opening day there was a queue stretching for two blocks, for doughnuts! They had created a sense of rarity and uniqueness that made people feel like they had to have one, or a dozen as it turned out. Now they are everywhere, and they have completely lost their unique spark. But even though there was nothing particularly special about their doughnuts, they marketed them in such a way as to make them look like no other doughnut, thus making people want the special unique doughnut. Market what you do or sell as a one of a kind and unique, and if you think there is nothing unique about what you do, think about doughnuts.

There are many ways to create rarity and uniqueness.

Once there was an old man who held in his possession a rare and ancient scroll believed to be only one of two left in existence. Because of their scarcity, they were said to be worth over a million dollars each. The old man, after much deliberation, made a dramatic decision to publicly destroy the scroll. Why would he do this?

Because he also had the other scroll, and he knew its value would be more than triple should it be the last one of its kind in existence.

Create a sense of uniqueness. I'm not saying you publicly destroy a part of your inventory, but you need to start thinking about what it is that you can offer your customer to set them apart from their competitors. Or if you are dealing with an end user, show them how they will be different from their neighbors.

This is also an excellent tie in for your close if there is competition. I will go in to this in the closes chapter but for now, think about whatever is unique about your product or service, promote that as a point of difference and then come time to close the sale, if you are not looking to close there and then, say "now I know you are going to look around and compare products, it's the smart thing to do (telling them to do what they will already do makes you look on top of their game) you need to consider, the main thing is …(and your unique point)" tell them to look around, but to compare what you know is unique about your product. This close can also focus on the strength of your product or service, not just its uniqueness.

Create a unique product. There is something different about what you sell, even if it is just where it is made, you can build a history up on that town.

Before you get on to the next chapter, take five minutes to jot down five things that make what you sell completely different to what the competition does.

Is there anything at all unique about your service that no one else does quite in the same way?

Do you offer a different color?

Is it European? Anything at all

Remember.

Unique.

14 Don't be the smartest person in the room

The old way of thinking was to always be the smartest person in the room.

I saw this line in a movie recently that had this exact same phrase in it "always be the smartest person in the room". In the films defense, it was about a bunch of magicians who plan a bank robbery, so being the smartest in the room may keep you from being locked up. But if you are with your associates, customers or prospects, this way of thinking is egotistical and arrogant. Why on earth would you want to be smartest in the room?

You will not be able to learn anything, and everyone else in the room will look to you for answers. You won't need to ask questions. On the other hand, if you know you aren't smartest in the room, you will proudly ask for advice. You will have the freedom to put your hands up and say, "Anyone got any ideas on this one".

Henry Ford was once accused by the press of not knowing anything about cars, he then proposed a Q&A for the non-believers. Ford then sat at a board room table with his pen on hand and a phone in front of him, he took all the questions the reporters could throw at him while he jotted them all down. When they were done with the questions, he put down the pen and picked up the phone and preceded to call his engineers. One by one, he got the answers he needed.

All you need to know is about your business and theirs, never concern yourself knowing everything and having all the answers or being more intelligent than the next person.

You should be the one asking all the questions. Sure you should be the expert in your field, or at least know the best way to solve their problems, but never think for a moment you need to have every answer. There is no shame in finding a solution through the guidance of others. In fact the opposite is true. You will gain far more respect by using your team, than you would being the lone wolf. No man is an island. There is no such thing as a self-made millionaire. Everyone needs help, and when you show others you know who to ask and how to get the correct answers, you will show the world you have the strength to move beyond your own self-pride.

If you are with your associates, customers or prospects, this way of thinking is egotistical and arrogant.

Don't be the smartest person in the room.

You will only feel lonely and drained. Get help, we need help. People need people who also need people.

Remember

Smartest

15 The Devil's Advocate

The term 'Devil's Advocate' was coined in a process once used by the Roman Catholic Church called Canonization. Canonization is the process of declaring a deceased person a Saint, so as to appear on a list of saints called the Canon List or just 'The Canon'. The church employed a promoter of the faith called a Devil's Advocate. They were a lawyer, or a cannon lawyer, hired to argue against the canonization of recently dead prospective. It was the job of this Devil's Advocate to look at a candidate with a skeptical view. To look for character faults and the like. For the sole reason of keeping the list of saints down to the deserved few.

Before this method of using the Devil's Advocates', virtually anyone could be nominated as a Saint and find a listing on the Canon.

If we play a small role in one or two negatives, our potential customers will trust us as an authority on the subject. It's for this reason we should look at adopting the Devil's Advocate on the sales meetings. Not to stop those unworthy from finding sainthood, but rather to provide an impartial or unbiased argument for any and all ideas. More on that later.

So why would we need to nominate a person to do this role?

That's a great question, who said that?

We need to have an agreed by the team, nominated, devil's advocate because unfortunately, and especially in a group, we are either biased or cowards.

Yup, biased or cowards. To a degree that is. We are afraid of many a thing in a meeting, and if we voice up against a co-workers idea, we run the risk of being shot down and have a stapler thrown at us at best. At worst, the boss would like to have a word with us in private. This makes us cowards in the long run. Or on the other hand we may be biased, and if this is the case we will not listen to the ideas objectively enough to provide negative feedback for the ones that may not work. We would see the ideas through rose colored glasses. When we appoint someone as the Devil's Advocate, and by the way, it needs to be a different person every week, to give variety with all the necessary objections and so we don't create an enemy. We will have created a sort of third party to sit in and look for all the reasons something may not work. Provided they know their role and they have good ability to assume the other argument. They will look past the benefits and advantages. They will look for the faults. They will be the ones at the back saying "what about the transport costs?" and "we don't have the man power" or "that's not legal" Whatever they come up with is purely to stimulate thought in all directions, rather than straight up. Devil's Advocates can be incorporated in to the negative as well, like a decision to fire a group, or a meeting to plan a punishment. It is just an opposing person, delegated to provide a difference of opinion.

> *Unfortunately, and especially in a group, we are either biased or cowards.*

If we are to have a representation of all thoughts in a meeting we need to provide a model to support it. Like any well-structured meeting, we have a minute taker, a time keeper, a presenter or meeting head and now a devil's advocate.

Try this for your next meeting, not a training meeting, rather a meeting where you would normally come up with ideas and plans for changes. You will be surprised at the things one will come up with when appointed devil's advocate.

Remember

Devil

16 Bargaining

You are at a meeting with a client. All the specifics are discussed and agreed upon. The technical information is explained and the quality has nods all round, and then they say,

"So what can we do about the price then, it's just too expensive"

To where the old school salesman would say something like

"Where do we have to be?"

Or "what figure did you have in mind?"

Or even worse, "I'll give you another 10% but that's all I can do".

I'm going share a very simple phrase with you now that will put the bargaining argument to bed, because there are only three reasons you should lower your price, only three.

Quantity, terms, and loyalty.

Quantity. If the customer agrees to buy ten times the amount, then you need to look after them. This is your tool, not theirs. It's a bargaining chip you bring out when the topic is brought up by the customer and you need to say yes we can lower the price if we raise the quantity.

> *When we look at someone who has something we want, we see them as having something better than us.*

Terms, if they are willing to pay sooner rather than later, its money in the bank and the interest alone will tell you to look after them. This is your tool, not theirs. The only reason they will offer sooner payment is to lower the price, there is no other reason a business would want to off load. Unless there is something else at play, like a tax problem or end of year budget like a government agency will have. If this is the case, a few more questions will soon bring this to light. Questions like "will paying sooner help you guys out?"

Finally, Loyalty. If they have been a regular for twenty years, take care of them. This is how the Chinese do business, well, historically it has been. Years of trading has a lot of influence for some people, especially family businesses and longtime trading businesses. Protect this plant where you can, because as it grows, it may be the only thing keeping your competitors at bay.

In order for you to truly understand the phrase that will stop the price beaters dead in their tracks, you need to understand in your own mind why we buy. I am going to share the phrase with you in a moment, but first answer me this question.

Why do we buy things?

I know it's a kind of vague question but it really has only one answer, and that is this. We buy things because we believe what we want is worth more than the value of the money.

We want the goods or service more than we want the money we have worked so hard for. That money is valuable to us, and it is our money.

Here is an interesting thought process. When we look at someone who has something we want, we see them as having something better than us, and we are willing to trade our own valuables with them. We see them as luckier, as we would someone with a new toy or a hot new partner. This is not jealousy nor is it envy. It's more of a mixture of admiration and desire. We see them as one step ahead of us and we want to be where they are, with what they have.

Keeping this in mind as a buyer, even if you truly believe this thing you are buying may be worth less, by asking the seller if you can have it for less money, you are asking for a trade in value. Without a reason for this trade like "the tires need replacing" or "there is a tear in the fabric", what you are saying is that you believe what they have is not as valuable as they think it is. Some make a living bargaining for goods and this may be second nature to them, but to some, this may be a little insulting. Especially if there is no real reason for you asking for less other than you want to pay less. So this little one liner can be used in exactly the same way for sellers and buyers alike. Whether you are trying to reduce your buy price or keep a high selling price you can say to either your vendor or purchaser.

"I haven't got any more money to give you"

As a buyer, by saying you haven't got any more money to give them, you are not risking insult by sending the message of less worth. All you are saying is that's all you have to give, and if they want a sale, here is what you have to exchange. I have seen an excellent example of this in a home sale where the buyer offered an odd amount for a home $372.685.80, to illustrate that's all they had in the world to offer. That sort of offer sure stops any counter offer.

As a seller you are illustrating to the buyer the item of value is an item of value to you to and not just something you want money for. When you say to a buyer you have no more money to give them, something in them changes and you can see it in an instant. Their chin pushes up and they raise their eyebrows in an expression of agreement, and they seem to understand in an instant.

Use the phrase "I haven't got any more money to give you" and you can continue on with the purchase and selling process knowing the issue of value has been addressed.

Remember

Moneyless

17 Set a goal for yourself, not a budget

Goal setting really should have its own book all together. For now though, we will have a quick look at basic goal setting 101.

Goal setting is the foundation for all your plans and future endeavors. Without a goal you are simply relying on things to fall in to place, although sometimes you may need more than just a goal, but I'll explain more on that in the next chapter.

So what has this got to do with the out with the old and in with the new theme? Well, we used to call them budgets in the good old days. And all they did was stress you out and give the boss something to tell you off about. A budget focuses on an abstract figure of a represented growth for your work, and is just too hard to get an honest emotional good feeling about. How can we get excited about a budget when the numbers are the sole focus? We need a tangible goal to feel something. We need a motorcycle, a car or a new TV for making ten new accounts last month. Just making budget for the month and getting a $400 bonus will never get you out of bed like a new fishing rod in the shop window, or that new games console for the family. How about if you make the month's quota, you can go to the snow for the weekend. We need to look at what will drive us to wake up one hundred mornings and say let's do this, and I have to say a budget alone, will not achieve this level of motivation.

Start right now. Get a pen and right down a list of ten things you want. Anything from a new pair of shoes to a lady for the night to a speed boat or a log cabin in the woods. What do you dream about? What do you want when you see it in a window of a shop or on TV? A backyard pool? A new mountain bike? These are the goals that you need to get to paper right now, go for it!

Ok so we have a few things to focus on. This will change over time to be sure, but for now we have something to work with. Now go over the list and pick the one you want and need the most of all. Then go ahead and rank them all from what you want the most to the least.

Now let's focus on the first three things. Of the three, which would you be most likely to achieve the soonest. That is your primary goal for the next six months. If you think you can get it in less time, that's great, but we need something we can build a plan with, something we can have the time to develop some good habits with. It takes around a month to make or break any habit and another month to create routines around that habit so we need a few months at this.

Now to truly get this going, make some post-it notes, photos, or magazine cutouts of the thing you are focusing on and place them around the house and your work place.

The final stage is to have a rock solid plan of how you are going to get this thing you want. If you are wanting a new boat in the next six months. Have a plan to get to that exact money you need within the next twenty four weeks. If the boat is $5k you will need to save or make an extra $208 each week for the next twenty four weeks.

> *What do you dream about? What do you want when you see it in a window of a shop or on TV?*

Write this down and keep looking at your goal every day. Keep an eye on your progress, and be happy knowing you are getting closer and closer every day.

Remember the goal must be small enough to be achievable within a relatively short time frame. If the goal is too big and is too far away, it will act as a demotivation and you will begin to give yourself reasons why not to do it.

For me, my greatest motivation is my family. I tell them my goals and they remind me every day, especially if it involves them. We currently have a goal for a new home laptop for the family to use. Every time we go shopping I show the kids the laptop we are getting and how much closer we are to it. They remind me every morning to transfer the saving money to the laptop fund.

Goal setting will help. It will give you focus and clarity. It will allow you to build up something every day and help keep you motivated. But unfortunately as I personally found out, sometimes, goal setting may not be enough.

Remember

Goal

18 A goal may not be enough

If you were to go to any number of wealth building, future planning or life coaching seminars they will all tell you the first thing you need to do is to get a goal. Figure out what you want and write it down. Then come up with a plan to get it. A good, well thought out plan to achieve your goal.

Say you want to earn 10% more income. You work out a monthly, six monthly and yearly plan to achieve it. Or you want a new car, or a new home, any goal is achievable with a good plan in your goal setting. Quit smoking, lose weight you name it you can achieve it. So why do so many of us not reach our goals. Why can we not find the willpower and discipline to make it happen when deep down, after all the planning we know we can?

The reason is, we have no reason. We have not got a big enough why.
One can overcome almost any how, if they have a big enough why.
Garry Zancanaro, founder of SelfImprovementDirectory.com says, *"It is vital to know WHY we want whatever it is we want, because it's our 'whys' that determine the strength of our desire, and our ultimate success in achieving our goals. Without a big enough 'why' our chances of success in reaching any goal are greatly reduced."*

Say you wanted to set a goal to travel to Paris in the summer just to see the Eifel Tower because you have never been overseas and like the sound of France in the summer.

Alternatively, your child falls ill and the only chance for their survival is a lifesaving operation in France within the next three months.

Of these two whys, which do you think will stand a better chance of success in raising the funds needed for the travel to France? I personally know of at least two people that have always wanted to go overseas, but have never had a strong enough why.

We need a rock solid reason for the goal or we will simply give up when the going gets tough.

In sales it is no different. It is common for someone in sales to have a budget or a sales target. It is also common for that target to be consistently within a few percent of the one hundred percent mark, give or take. When the goal is big enough, the sales person will smash the target, time and time again. They will find a way.

Get a goal and then get a why. You can of course get a why and then look for a goal to match. If you want to travel around Australia, you may want to buy a motor home, thus your new goal is a Winnebago.

> *If it is a sales target you are chasing, set the personal goal for ten percent higher, and give yourself a reward when you get it.*

Some of the bigger goals like smoking gambling or weight loss are all in the same boat. We have all had or have a big goal we have never seemed to be able to reach. Try this little experiment. Mind map the goal. Write the goal in the center of a blank piece of paper. From there, begin writing all the reasons you want that to happen, kids, quality of life etc. then from that break it down deeper, so if you wrote kids then write say playing cricket on Sunday.

This is one of my mind maps as an example.

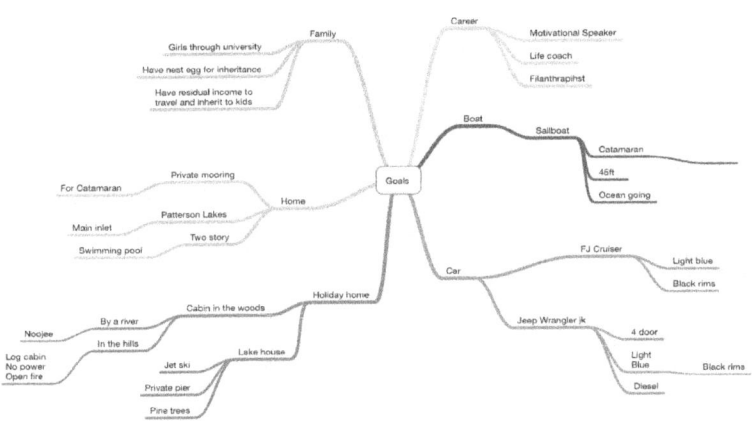

Start off small and try this for yourself. If it is a sales target you are chasing, set the personal goal for ten percent higher, and give yourself a reward when you get it. Something you really want, like a new TV, a weekend away, or a day with the kids at a theme park. Whatever it is, it needs to be a deep down desire that keeps you going.

Like I said in the previous chapter, this is not a book on goal setting. So what I'm going to do is share five of my favorites with you.

1, The Magic Lamp: Goal Setting for People Who Hate Setting Goals by Keith Ellis

2, Goal Setting 101: How to Set and Achieve a Goal! by Gary Ryan Blair

3, Goal Setting: How to Create an Action Plan and Achieve Your Goals (Worksmart) by Michael Singer Dobson

4, Write It Down, Make It Happen: Knowing What You Want and Getting It by Henriette Anne Klauser PhD

5, Eat That Frog!: 21 Great Ways to Stop Procrastinating and Get More Done in Less Time by Brian Tracy

Get a goal, then get a big fat why for that goal and you will be unstoppable!

Remember,

Reason.

19 Set a sales goal for your customers

The old way of a salesman would be to set a target or sales goal for each customer. Typically this would only be between the sales person and their superior. Imagine if you shared this goal with the customer, not so much as a financial goal, but more as a business development goal.

This is the new way a sales consultant would work. We (by this stage in the book, you are well and truly a consultant) would consult with the customer. We would talk about their business future and our role in it, thus concreting your position with them. A salesman would just be interested in how many units the customer purchases. A consultant is interested in how they are selling them or consuming them, what they have planned for the disposal of them once they are done and if they can even help in the sales process to their customers. A good sales consultant (like you and I) will have a twelve month plan for the customers they deal with. Even a barber shop needs a plan for their customers. As simple as next week I will trim that fringe again and your ears will be once per two months, nose hairs, next month.

> *A good sales consultant (like you and I) will have a twelve month plan for the customers they deal with.*

Get a game plan in place for your customers and they will be so taken aback by your forethought, professionalism and open planning they will want to keep you around for financial security

Remember

Goals

20 You're not as important as they are

The traditional salesman would wear a suit, have a well thought out power tie and sport gold cuff links, all in the name of self-promotion. When we see a salesman in a suit with a gold watch and a leather brief case we immediately think he is trying to get one over on us by up classing us. On the contrary, if we simply dress respectably and focus on making the customer the more important ones, we will have a far easier time on the sale.

Think about how you felt, if you have ever had a salesman in a smart looking suit, in your home while you sit there in your tracksuit and mockies. It makes you feel inferior, like they are the ones in charge and you have the honor of dealing with them. That might sound great to some of you, but I'm sorry to say, you are not going to get the sort of partnership you need to make it to the relationship.

What you really need to be aiming at is a level, eye to eye type of feeling in the room. No one is better, ever. Some people are better at some things but no one is a better person. Like a tree is a tree, not better or worse than another tree, different species and looks, but still a tree. You are a human being, like every other human. So forget the different status levels and struggle for respect using Rolex and Armani, start by letting them know they are important.

I'm going to break it down in to a few little considerations for you to adopt, day by day, as you see fit. Take your time with these.

Read one, let it sink in, and look for a situation to apply it to someone you wish to feel important.

Step one. Accept people the way they are.

What psychologists call, unconditional positive regard, is simply you accepting someone just the way they are. It is a flaw of human nature to be judgmental and critical. We need to understand that we all cop judgment where ever we go and whomever we meet. If you can be that one person in their life who does not judge them, they will immediately show you their acceptance in return.

Step two agree with them.

Whatever they have to say, it is important to them and they believe what they are saying so hear it out and agree with what they are saying. When they are finished, if you still deep down disagree with them, just ask them what makes them say that, or why they feel that way. Do not raise you eyebrows, cross your arms or roll your eyes. Say to yourself you believe what they are saying simply because they believe in what they are saying, and understand they have seen different things and lead a different life that has made them feel that way. Consider this, if you had led the same life as them, would you not feel the same way too?

Step three

Show your appreciation for them.

Everyone in the world has a choice in what they do every day. They choose to get up in the morning, (most teenagers choose not to get up in the morning). They choose to go to work. They choose to give up their valuable time to spend it with you. Thank them for their time. Let them know you are grateful for their email response. Show people you understand they have a choice to deal with you, and they have chosen to give you their time. You appreciate that.

Step 4

Show your admiration

Everyone on the planet can do something better than you can. Everyone has a talent or skill they can beat you on. Think about every person you know and go through all the things you know you can do until you get to something they can do better. I guarantee you will be surprised at how quickly you come to something. It's quite humbling to realize you are not as good as anyone at something, yet you are better than everyone at something. Even a six month old baby can sleep in any environment, no matter the noise level, and can throw up on whomever they choose. A talent I truly do admire!

Step 5

Listen inventively.

Don't just wait for your turn to speak. Listen to what they have to say without trying to fill in the blanks or finish their sentence. When they have said what they wanted to say, make it a habit to wait for at least two seconds after they have finished talking, before you begin. They may have more to say and you will not run the risk of interrupting them. Start this today. When someone is talking to you, wait for two seconds of silence before beginning to speak. This ensures two things. One, you will be forced to listen without interruption and two it shows them you are really considering what they have just said.

Step 6

Don't criticize, condemn or complain

I learnt this the hard way, as I'm sure we all have a story to tell on this one. Several years ago I complained about a co-worker and the word got back to them about my problems with them. Needless to say there was tension between us and he never trusted me again, regardless of how I explained to them the Chinese whispers twisted my words, and the worst thing about it, as I'm sure you have seen again, I truly didn't feel that way anyway, the person who relayed the message was criticizing them and I just jumped on the band wagon, it was entrapment I tell you!. Don't get dragged in to a bitching session with anyone.

Whatever you think about someone has nothing to do with anyone. The same is said for them. Whatever others think about you, has nothing to do with you. Great minds talk about ideas, medium minds talk about events and small minds talk about people.

Step 7

Be the Good three Cs' Courteous, concerned and considerate.

This is just good old fashioned manners, please and thank you. How is the leg? How's the family? Think Mary Poppins and Hank from Driving Miss Daisy.

Open the door for people. Make a habit of offering your seat to women and opening doors for people. As a part of listening inventively, be concerned with what they are saying. It's important to them so treat it so. Be considerate to what they have to go through every day as well. Do they have traffic, kids or a boss? Do they have a death in the family or an ill family member? You don't know until they tell you and they may never tell you so just understand they have problems like everyone else does, and I'll bet you whatever their problems are, you wouldn't trade yours for theirs. Be courteous, concerned and considerate.

Live your life with these seven ideas as a starter and you will be well on your way to making people feel like they are number one when they are around you. When they feel like they are number one, the fear they had turns in to a feeling of power and control, and guess what happens then. They begin to develop the confidence to make the big decisions that used to scare them when they felt smaller around the scary salesman.

This entire chapter is really about putting yourself in their shoes. When you can have a true empathy and understanding like I have been harping on about for the entire book, you will be able to forget the word sales, and just think purchase order. (Too much?)

Make people feel important and they will remember admire and want you to work with them.

Remember

Importance

21 It isn't numbers game

I used to believe, as I'm sure you did too, that the sales industry is as simple as numbers equals results. The more people you prospect, meet with, and present your sales pitch, the better your odds of getting the job done and selling your share.

It was all about the group vs you as a sales person, and the united they stand divided they fall theory. Unless you have a few on your side in which case it's united they are with you. Well, that was true to a degree, though the rules have changed a lot in the last ten years with the emergence of social media.

I'll explain what I mean.
I was once the proud photographer and seller of my photographs on a day cruise ferry. People would buy a ticket for the boat and walk the ramp to the loading deck of the boat, upon where I would great them and take a picture of the happy holiday makers. I would then have it developed, and framed in a lovely cardboard frame, hey, it was lovely. I would then meet up with the same people on the boats return to offer the picture of them for sale. This would all work well, take a photo of someone, frame it and sell it back to them. The more people I could photograph, the more I could potentially sell, it's just numbers right? Wrong. It would all go so well until one of them said no to me, either on the way up the ramp, or as I was walking around selling the finished product. I would say politely, "ok, no photo for you, next please", and guess

what, they would say no as well, then the next one and the next one and so on, they would see someone say no and then think it was the norm or the thing to do. The only way to break free was to walk away from the group in question and come back to them later, or stop the flow of people walking up the ramp and wait a moment, as if there was a delay on the boat, surprisingly this did work sometimes. What was happening here was a combination of a group mentality, follow the leader, and a mirror neuron response reaction, like a yawn or a scream. The group mentality is what happens when we adopt the attitude that, if everyone else is doing it, I should too.

This was first measured a few decades ago when a small town was growing too fast, and in an effort to save power in the small growing community on the edge of the power grid, where the supply was becoming a problem, the authorities decided to take the following action.

> *It's not the numbers that will see you through, it's the product that will save you.*

Three letters where delivered in the neighborhood to all its residents. The first read saving power saves money, the second read saving power saves the environment, and the third read save power because all your neighbors are doing it. The first two letters had little or no reaction. People being told to do something just doesn't work if there is little incentive or punishment. The third letter however, revived an impressive reduction to power saving. Around two thirds less in fact. Why was this so?

If we see a crowd gathered, we want to investigate, knowing it is usually something we have seen before. When a group reacts to an event or task, we are naturally going to try to follow suit. It's in our nature, we are evolved from communal primates, not loners like bears. It there is something in your life you do not completely understand or believe in, is a safe bet that if everyone else is doing it, so shall you. Religion, sports codes and going to parties all have the same basis of group mentality. We can call it culture if we want to sound a little more sophisticated, but it's still 'follow the group'. "We are all doing it" will always have a better reaction than "you may be the only one".

So how does this relate back to sales?

Imagine you are selling photos to a group and one in the crowd says they are rubbish and overpriced. Instantly instilling doubt in to the rest of the group. You can go on all day long, but once the damage is done it's done. Tar and feathers are hard as hell to get off.

The solution is not to fight the numbers. If you try and solve the problem with marketing in this day and age, people will only attack you more. The word has spread, and the world of the social network has moved faster than you can. Once cursed, it's not a numbers game anymore.

It's not the numbers that will see you through, it's the product that will save you.

A number of years ago Coca-Cola released a drink called Mother. The first formula bombed, no one liked it, and overnight the entire market agreed the drink was bad. I remember myself choosing not to buy it because everyone said it was supposed to be terrible, but I never did try it, in fact this was the case for a lot of people. They didn't even bother to taste it. Once it was decided it was no good, it never stood a chance. Then in a stroke of genius, Coca-Cola made a slight change to the flavor and ran an ad campaign heading the slogan "we are sorry for the old Mother" the add went on to show a SWAT team storming a laboratory to arrest the chemists responsible for the failure. This brilliant reversal was the perfect reaction to what was an initial flop. They agreed with the crowd, they stood in alongside them and carried their own torches and pitchforks, metaphorically speaking. Them there chemists were the bad guys. Now try out this new one, the correct one from those of us alongside you good people. They joined them in their decision, and offered a solution, and so can you. Once the crowd has spoken the numbers become irrelevant. We take a step back and approach from the side wearing their colors.

All you need is an option, a second choice for them. The solution in the end for the photography job was to say, "no problem, here is your fee photo token for the cruise. I'll collect it later on the way over". Once the crowd decided they were not going to pose on the gangway that was that. Usually the token got a better photo anyway, but we needed to offer the first option to get the second, to make it their choice. It's not just a numbers game. We need to continually re-adjust our flight path. Trying out different solutions and offers when the group says no.

When it was decided the original mother formula didn't take. Coca-Cola didn't increase advertising and marketing. They knew additional numbers would not fix the issue. What had to be done was agree with them and offer a variation. They didn't even change the name. Doing this would admit a complete stuff up. All they did was change it a little and ride on the familiar 'Mother' brand name.

When you are finding you are having trouble increasing the sales or you are falling behind, or hey, just when you have an objection you can't use or deal with. Make a point of either using your own version of the 'feel, felt, found' method. I know how you feel, I felt the same way, and this is what I found. Or simply agree with them and show them the 'better' one.

> *We need to continually re-adjust our flight path. Trying out different solutions and offers when the group says no.*

Work smarter, not harder. Starting again takes so much longer than a rebrand, and if you want to hit the ground running after a setback, the best thing you could do for yourself and your business is to change it up and offer a remix. After all, there is no such thing as bad publicity right, so why not use that awareness to your advantage. Next time you have a brick wall, a flop, or a dead end, don't keep throwing money at it thinking the marketing will help, and don't ditch it all together either. Look for another way to build upon what your customer already knows.

Remember

Numbers

22 Why should they buy from you

Back in the day, and by that I mean the way back in the nineties, there was a person called a sales representative, heard of them? They visited customers and prospects offering items typically unique to the business they represented. If you wanted to purchase a brand name item you would have to either meet with the rep or pay retail prices. The only other choice was perhaps a wholesaler, but you would have to purchase in bulk, have a minimum spend account or some other condition.

As I keep saying throughout this book, selling has changed, because buying has changed.
Today people not only have an abundance of choice when it comes to goods and services, they also have an abundance of choice for where and who they get any given goods or service from. eBay, Gum Tree, Trading post and the list goes on, admittedly petering off to the smaller online merchants. Multinational corporations and e-commerce companies, are providing consumer-to-consumer business-to-business and business-to-consumer sales for just about anything you could imagine and require. I personally have stood in front of a

> *The interesting thing about telling people to shop around, is it usually stops them shopping around.*

customer who has taken out their phone as I have finished my demonstration of a product, and shown me the exact product I had in my hand, available to them online, for less than my cost price. How can we fight that, why should anyone buy from you when they have such fantastic choice of vendors. The thing that makes you different is you, and only you can answer what that may be.

What would people get from you if they did business with you, that they would not get if they purchased the goods electronically? Would the service be better? More support perhaps? As I said only you can answer that.

So what you need to do now to fight the digital free-for-all is to highlight the benefits only you can provide, and make sure they will look at your benefits as a priority by **making** them a priority. You do this by telling them, it is the most important thing about the thing they are buying. Sounds silly but it's true.

People will take it on board if you tell them, when they shop around, make sure they are going to get the after service and warranty. Or when they compare prices, are they looking at the training and support with that price. Whatever your strong point is, sell your item on that, and tell the customer to consider that when they shop around.

The interesting thing about telling people to shop around, is it usually stops them shopping around. Just like Bunnings tells us they will beat any advertised price by 10% thus making us feel they have the cheapest prices to begin with. Telling people to compare your strongest feature will subconsciously put that at the top of their list. Nine times out of ten they will appreciate your confidence, and just buy from you anyway.

What is your strength?

What do you have that no one in your field does?

Tell your customers they need to consider this when they look around.

Remember,

Strength.

23 Don't overcome objections

What are the objections we have been taught to overcome?

Before you keep reading, jot down at least four objections you face regularly, more would be better.

Now look at those objections in depth, what are they really objecting to? What are they really saying to you in those objections?

Interestingly, the only two objections are in fact the only two emotions, FEAR and LOVE.

Think now of all the objections you have ever had.
"I don't want to change brands", fear of change.
"I'm happy with my current product", either love for the brand name creating a bias that's bad for business, or again fear of change.
"I know this one I'm buying now works and my people know it". This is a fear of your product not filling the shoes and things going south.

"My brother's mate's mother is going to look after me". Love, this is a tough one that only time and trust will help you to get over.

"I need approval from the manager", assuming they do have the authority, this is fear of making the call themselves.

"The timing is not right". Again this is a fear of change and it is just them procrastinating.

"It's too expensive" Fear of making a buying mistake in paying too much.

Any objection you can think of has its foundations in most cases with fear, and love will occasionally show its head here, though usually fear is the captain of the "No thanks". Going back to how we talked about it in chapter six, and all the things people go through when making a big decision, doesn't it make sense to help them through their decisions rather than trying to rational them with facts. After all, if you had a fear of spiders, snakes or heights, no amount of facts on the non-venomous and placid natured huntsman spider and carpet python will stop the chills and shakes you feel when they are placed on your hand. Nor the engineers certificates on the safety of a suspended structure hundreds of meters in the air.

Would you hold a pet like this?

Or this

Or perhaps a glass viewing platform like this

None of these fears could ever be overcome with reason and facts. Only understanding, trust, and empathy will work.

Just as a fear of snakes may be over overcome with gradual exposure to pictures and then the same room then a small snake on a table and so on. We can work through any objection, and when we take the time to do it well, we will have an unbreakable link that will see our partnership flourish and referrals flood in.

So where do we start then?

The first step is, we need to learn to use the objection as the motivation. If they have a fear of change, then explain how the world is going to change around them and tell them about the place down the road who didn't change and now they have foreclosed.

If they don't want to try the new product because it may not work tell them a story about two customers, one who tried it and prospered and one who didn't and floundered. Use their own fear as a motivation for their success.

The second step is to walk them through their doubts. As with the gradual exposure to a snake starting with pictures, if the fear is great we need to take care and let them take time to understand it will all work out for the better. Remember the starting point for all this is trust. Without trust none of this will work, so I'm going to assume you have their trust. Then we need to introduce a small part of what we do. We can do this by saying something like this. "Mr. Customer, I can appreciate you may not have the faith that my product can do the job, would you give me a small opportunity to prove to you just how good it is and how well it will work for you, because if you do (because, always use because to explain) you will see greater profits and happier clients". Of course choose your own words. Just use the principle of offering a small piece, if you can, if you can't then a trial or test drive. If you can't do that, then a massive open door and cooling off. Always add the "because if you do", I can't stress how well it works on easing peoples tension. When you say because to someone, in fact try it on your partner or friends. Tell them something absurd like pigs can't look up. Then say because, they have a spine like ours and it's like us looking up from our hands and knees. (Say dogs can't because big Al said they can't.) You could tell them you can grow forty different types of fruits on a single tree, because Dr. Sam Aken is an art professor at the University Of Syracuse, in America and he grafted a tree of forty fruit. Say you understand why they object and it's the objection that's the reason to move "can't afford it, that's why you need it", give them a smaller trial option and say because, then a fact why.

Use objections as the reason to buy.

Remember

Objections

24 Not everyone can sell

There is a funny de-motivational poster with a picture of a hurdles jumper falling over the hurdle, below there is a caption that reads, *winners never quit and quitters never win, but if you never quit and never win you're a loser.*

The old school will tell you anyone can learn the skills to be a great salesperson. I used to believe this to be true, that anyone could develop the skills to become great. That may have been the case many years ago when pitches and closes still had the effect that knowledge and trust has today. Now though, no matter how much training some people get, it's just not in them to be great at selling. Now there are naturals out there that have a knack for making people feel comfortable dealing with them, and some others need to learn and hone the skills necessary to be great. Of course anyone who receives training will improve, just as anyone can learn a sport and get good through practice. The training they get will always help them to a degree, but there is a limit for some, and no matter how much they train, the gold medal is just not for them, there is a limit on their ability. This may seem to go against everything your parents or a motivational speaker will tell you. They will say you can be and do whatever you want. That is simply not true. We can't all be doctors, lawyers, astronauts or great sales professionals. Now I'm not looking to carry on about how there is a special place for the great sales force of the world and all others can kneel before Zod. My message here is this, learn the basics of sales, read books, go to seminars and listen to audio books and love what you do. If you find you are struggling for every sale and fearing the phone after several years in sales. If you feel like it is hard work and you are still hating the sales role even though you have tried a few different companies, then there is no shame in quitting. Learning to quit at the right time instead of going through years of pain will see you a better life. This is the one and only life you have, so why not do something you enjoy and have a natural talent at. Not everyone can be a great sales person though some of us love it and choose to stay in the profession and that's great. I can't sail a boat if my life depended on it (on occasion it has) but I love it and I'll keep sailing till I die (probably trying to sail).

> *This is the one and only life you have, so why not do something you enjoy and have a natural talent at.*

Please understand, this is not a quitting request form. In no way am I suggesting you hang up the business card and pull the pin because you aren't that good and the work is hard. Anything worth doing is going to be hard work, and if you have never read the books and done the training, chances are you can improve your skills, so give it time and commit twelve to twenty four months of solid work and building your skills. If at the end of two years full, and I say FULL, book a month, daily audio and monthly seminars commitment, you still suck at sales and hate it, then move on to what you love. There are many a professional turned vineyard owner or artist. Life is too short for bad career choices.

Do what you love, love what you do, and quit what you suck at!

Remember,

Quit

25 Don't go straight for the Relationship

The old way is all about beginning with a good relationship.

Q, What is the foundation to a solid sales area?

A, "A strong sales area always begins with good relationships. It's all about relationships."

Bzzzz, wrong. At least not in the beginning.

Don't try to get them to be your friends, this is so old school it's corny. Salesmen calling people mate and pal. Giving them nick names and inviting them to golf days before they have even bought anything. All this does is make the customer feel obliged or seduced in to the sales process. The sales person looks too desperate, and it makes them look like they have no other options in the bag other than gifts and besties.

Every day I hear business owners and manager's alike saying how hard it is to find a reliable, honest, hardworking person.

Of course back in the day this was a good thing to do. Traditionally people would not want to do business with someone who wasn't their mate or their mates mate. We liked doing business with friends because they could teach us all the details we needed to know and we had no other way of getting that information without studying it for days. Now the information is at

109

their fingertips and they have three hundred friends on Facebook, so why would they need a salesperson to be their pal? They don't. We shouldn't try to be their pals, a least not at the start. Ever had a sales person call you mate or buddy or even worse, a nick name. I get Dan or Danny. I love telling them its Daniel or Mr Marshall, puts them back in their suit and tie.

If we as sales consultants should not look to befriend the people we are selling to, what are we to do? Where do we aim if not for a friendship?

We need to flip this on its head. If in the past they needed information, and from that they formed friendship and then a partnership, then now we take away the need for information. What are they looking for in the beginning?
What is the single hardest thing of any business? Whether you are building cars or baking bread, selling houses or selling loans. The hardest thing in any business in the world is finding good people to work with. If you have good people to work with, any business will work, have bad people and any business will fail. If that is the single hardest thing they are dealing with, then does it not make sense to be one of the good people they need to work with? Every day I hear business owners and manager's alike saying how hard it is to find a reliable, honest, hardworking person to take care of the things they cannot, and this, is where you step in.

Enter, the Partnership

The partnership is what we used to build up after the relationship was formed after a customer sought information.
We used to focus on being mates, get the business and then grow the business with them thus forming the partnership down the track.
Now it is the other way around, flipped over and ass over tits. We have to look at what they need, provide that level of service and support and then become the consultant and partner they need in their business. All the time building trust and respect, thus forming the friendship along the way so they will trust our information as good insight.

People today know the free pens and lunch doesn't help their business, and as nice as you may be, and hey, they may really like you all said and done, they are not going to do business with you if they believe you have not got what they need for their business to grow. You may get a few sales, and you will even get a coffee when you call on them, but if you do not focus on that partnership, there will come a day when you visit them and see your competitor's car in the car park or their product on the shelves.

Focus first on the partnership, then build to a friendship.

Create a strong partnership, and the relationship will naturally grow.

Remember

Partnership

26 What can you do for me

Ok here's what's going to happen, I'm going to slap you in the face with a sad little fact, and then I'm going to hold your hand and tell you I am sorry, I'll explain why I did it, and then I will ask you for your forgiveness.

Ok so here is the slap.

Your customers don't care about any of your methods or products.

They don't care for the strategies we discuss in meetings or the years of university education. Nor do they care for the R&D that has gone in to the products you sell or use. They care not for the love you have for what you sell, nor do they care for the pride you take in your service. They don't even care that you love your job.

I'm sorry, I'm sorry, I know it hurts but I had to say it. I had to tell you this because so many professional sales people believe their customers really care about what they do and why they do it.

Here's what they care about, and if you have ever bought something this is all you ever cared about as well.

All your customers care about is what can it do for them. That's all they want to know. What can your product or service do to make their life better in some way shape or form.

What do they want in what you have, that they are willing to give up their money for. In other words, they need to believe they will be better off with what you are offering, than they are with their hard earned cash.

The last time you bought a TV, did you care about the R&D that went in to it, no? Did you care about the school the mechanic went to when you got your car serviced, no? Now this may seem a little contradictive to the chapter on knowing their business and yours, it isn't for this reason. You need to know everything about your business and theirs, so when they do ask that one question that matters to them you will know the answer and look like a champion. Everything else they don't care about because it doesn't affect them.

We don't buy a drill because we want a drill, what we want is a hole. We look at what the thing we are going to pay for can give us.

As beautiful as a 9kt diamond ring is, I am not about to purchase one for myself regardless of the craftsmanship and the clarity. Though if there is a question such as "will you marry me?" lingering in the air, I may have a reason to look at what it can do for me.

What can the thing you are selling, do for the person you are looking to sell it to?

Here's a good little piece of information. When you find the need you will have your bullet proof close. Without that you are just trying to sell something to someone who may or may not need it and all your products advantages or your service methods will be unwanted.

Customers don't care about your methods or products. All they care about is what's in it for them. In a polite way, all your customers are selfish. As you and I are selfish when we are looking for something to buy. Keep this in mind and you will not lose yourself in your own product.

Remember

Selfish

27 Use yesterday's ideas today, and you'll be broke tomorrow

This heading could be used to sum up this entire book, and indeed be the title of the book, and that is why I have left it for the very end. (Well almost the end) It is the back bone of what I am writing about.

If we use the lessons of what we learnt yesterday in the fast changing world of today we will be left in the past. We are either moving forward, or we are moving backward, there is no in-between because the world is progressing. Even if we remain stationary, then we are falling behind.

In chapter nine I talked about the value of experience, well, I said it was useless, I guess I didn't really talk about it. Gaining this understanding that only principles are king, and the simple fact that yesterday's methods are as fickle as fashion will let you keep an open mind to the amazing changes taking place faster than they have ever been in the history of our existence.

We must continually learn and evolve our understanding of what works, and what does not. Talk to others in the industry, go to seminars, read books and listen to audio programs. Above all, try out new things.

Like a comedian trying new material for laughs, you need to constantly be on the trial and error page. Every day asking yourself, "what if I said this, or done that".

Your internal R&D department should be fully functional, and throwing out questions like what, how, who and where.

I'll keep this chapter short, only because the message here is a simple one. The past is the past and its platform is a little too distant for us to work off today. Look to the lessons within this book and keep an open mind. Yesterday will drain you of all your energy if you keep pushing the hard road, and the practices of the past are by far, a harder way of working.

> *We are either moving forward, or we are moving backward, there is no in-between because the world is progressing. Even if we remain stationary, then we are falling behind.*

Remember,
Past.

28 Sales and marketing are one in the same

There was a time, long long ago, when it was understood that the marketing department worked at the other end of the office, with separate agendas. Opposites in every way. The sales force (I always loved that term "Sales Force". The sales-force is ready for deployment to delta quadrant to destroy the pitchinions), had a budget to get to and the marketing team had a budget to stay under. Those in marketing would be trying gimmicky monthly campaigns and themes like movie titles and super hero campaigns. "The Super Hero super-deals week" to get ordinary items to look extra ordinary. This usually frustrated the sales professionals who only ever wanted to keep a level of professional sales. A little hard when you have to mention the crazy deal of the year created by a marketing person with very little knowledge of what is really going on in the field. And even worse in some cases. Like when I worked in one office where the marketing team and the sales people don't even talk to each other, and it's the customer that has the job of informing the campaign deal to the sales people. This lack of communication happens more than you might think.

Marketing and sales used to be different people. They used to be hired by different people and had two different views of the customer world. A sales person would see a customer as a life source and a potential boost. A marketing person would see a customer as a number, a set of eyes, just one of the hundreds of people looking at their ads. For the most part they never really got any kind of feedback for their work. The goal for the marketing team used to be, make it interesting and stick within the budget.

Ha, all this time, I have been saying in the past, when really it is still the case for some businesses today. Can you believe it? Some businesses have a separate marketing and sales department, ha.

This is the way it needs to work, for an effective sales process to take place. The sales team must understand and practice good marketing, and the marketing team must understand and practice good sales. They are two sides of the same coin.

> *The marketing team and the sales people don't even talk to each other, and it's the customer that has the job of informing the campaign deal to the sales people.*

We start with marketing. The marketing personal will have to have regular sales meetings and training, and attend all the same meetings as the sales team. They need to have a sales growth budget. I understand this may be a little hard when they are not selling directly, but if they are doing a campaign on a product, there needs to be a form of measurement associated with that. At a hydraulics place I worked at, the marketing manager had a single product budget that would change each month to match her campaign. This gave her a good incentive to communicate more with the sales team and get the feedback she needed to make the necessary changes. The sales team needs to have a great input as to what campaigns and products they wish to run with and for how long. They must understand marketing and appreciate the role it has in their job as sales people, indeed they need to know they are marketing every time they are talking to a customer.

Sales and marketing are one in the same. Without one the other will struggle in their role. They must work together, sell together and market together. Travel days with the sales team for the marketing team and office days with the marketing team for the sales people. Learning each other's jobs and what they can do to improve their own.

Sales and marketing are one in the same, so much so, that is what it should read in each other's business cards. When introducing themselves, "I'm in sales and marketing".

The fact is, a sales person is in marketing whether they want to be or not. Every time they hand out a card its marketing, the logo on their shirt, the stickers on their car, the shop front, the phone calls, it's all marketing, actually the only bit of sales they do is in the one meeting they might have to do the sale.

Sales and Marketing, like Frodo and Sam, Bonnie and Clyde or Tango and Cash, they are a team, and that's how they will work the best.

Remember

Marketing

29 Don't be the hardest working person in the office

Think about a place you have worked at, current or in the past, with a number of employees, say over ten or so. Now think of who may have been the hardest working person in that office. The one that always seemed to be slogging it out day after day.

A cleaner perhaps. Or a stores person. Chances are they are not the highest paid person. Chances are they are not constantly looking for an easier way of doing things, or a better way.

This is the person who believes hard work is the key to success. Now we know that to be untrue. I'm not suggesting you take it easy either, there is a balance and I'll get in to that in a moment. What I am saying is do not think for a moment that the only way to get ahead is to start early, finish late, and skip lunch. I have a friend who truly believes, the way to financial freedom is to work twelve hours a day, six days a week and commit your life to your career. This is just insanity. He will have a heart attack before he is fifty, if he's lucky.

Don't be the hardest working person in the office. If you find yourself staying back after everyone has left, ask yourself what you are doing that is so time consuming, and look to delegate or find a faster way.

As far as the other end of the scale, being a slacker won't get you any where either. Strive to be the most efficient person in your office, or even in your field. In the movie The Pursuit Of Happyness (spelt like the title, for all you spelling police) Will Smith's character realizes he has a smaller window of working hours to do the same job as all the other employees, and so he constantly looks for more efficient time savers like not hanging up the phone, rather use the hand on the dialer to click the leaver. Look for smarter ways to work. I have a laptop stand in my car that saves me time entering a call report after a customer call. Rather than leaving it on the passenger seat to falloff or in the bag and then opening it on my lap which surprisingly laptops are not very good on your lap.

What can you do to make your job easier and more efficient?

What can you do to ensure you are not the hardest working person in the office?

What is someone else doing that is a better way than the way you are doing?

The one who works the hardest is usually the lowest paid, and in a lot of cases, the least appreciated. Have you ever worked on a Sunday when no one else did, and all you got in return was a request to come in the following Sunday?

Strive to become the smartest worker, not the hardest worker.

Remember,

Worker.

30 Talk about Failure.

The old way will tell you to be positive and optimistic about what you are selling.

That failure is not an option!

If we adopt this attitude, failure becomes invisible, and so making is almost inevitable. We need to discuss the possibility that things may go wrong and the topic of discussion may not work.

Almost every sales meeting I have attended sees the topic of failure, left at the door. This is driven by fear and optimism (love). Now there is nothing wrong with either one of those emotions, as long as one can acknowledge them and act accordingly. Talking about the possibility of a failure allows you to think about the event and the actions you will take to avoid it. In Richard Branson's book, Losing My Virginity, he talks about all the stupid things he does to get ahead in the early days, and some of them are not so much stupid as illegal. I found myself saying 'why did he do that? I would have never done that!' All the time reinforcing the scenario in my own head. As I read about his failures and what came about as a result, I learnt what I must do to avoid them myself. This is what you must do in the office. Discuss the possibility of what might happen if. If the

> *Invite your customers to discuss the worst case events.*

shit hits the fan. If the service you provide doesn't meet the customers' expectations. Or if you simply need to raise the bar. Have you talked about failure enough, to know what you will do in as many conceived scenarios as possible?

Thinking about what we covered in the chapter about providing a Devil's Advocate, imagine combining a role like the Devil's Advocate to come up with as many crazy ways to fail as possible. You will not only see the possible failures of that meetings topic, you will be discussing events that are possible in any future dealing as well. Also, just so you are clear, the difference between this and the devil's advocate is, this is open to the table as a topic of conversation for any and all to talk about a possible failure scenario and what can be done to prevent it, whereas a devil's advocate will focus on why something won't work and should not be done, searching for objections at every turn, (much like my wife).

This is not just for your business meetings either. Invite your customers to discuss the worst case events as well. They will appreciate you having a broad view of the topic.

Talk about failure. Surprisingly, it will give you a certain peace of mind. We humans have a bad habit of burying worst case possibility's, especially in Australia. We love saying "yeah, she'll be right", and then we can't get to sleep. When we bring things out in to the open we tend to see them for what they really are and how they can really be handled.

I once had the opportunity for a large investment that scared the coins out of my bank account. After many a sleepless night wondering if I should go ahead or not, I decided to go camping to clear my head. I sat at a beautiful campsite that looked over a mountain range, as a trout filled river ran right through the camp site. I found myself thinking, wow, if this is as bad as it gets, I'm in. The investment was ok, not huge but definitely not the horror I dreamt of. We need to think of what would happen to us and our family should it all go south. If the risk for something like this is too big, re-consider. Otherwise, you only live once, no risk no reward and all that jazz.

Talk about failure. Only good will come of it. If it scares you to do so, then you may just be looking at things with rose colored glasses, and may not have given the venture enough thought to begin with.

If you still struggle with it, to level things out and provide an alternate perspective, ask a negative person what they think. We all know a few of them, co-workers, mother in law, that type of thing.

Talk about failure whenever you can. Who knows, you may even find yourself shining a light in the corner of your own fears you never knew you had.

Remember,

Failure.

31 What do you do

I'm going to ask you a question, and as I said I can hear you so feel free to answer out loud, just call out the answer.

The question is, what business are you in? Shoes! Shoes good. Car sales! Car sales, ok. Vegetarian! A what! Oh a Veterinarian, yep. Sorry one at a time, a hair salon, yep. Last one, Tyre shop! A Tyre shop, ok. Sorry if I missed you. Well, I have to say you are all wrong.

All the products and services you just told me are exactly that products and services. They are merely the things you deal in. They are the things you sell to make a living and honestly, if you changed your products or services a little or a lot, would you really change how you sell them that much?

You are not in the business of your products. You are in fact in the business of sales and marketing, research, distribution, accounting, customer management etc.

The sooner we can get a hold on that the sooner you can simply look at the overall picture of how you run your business, instead of get the stuff you sell to humans.

If McDonald's was to suddenly get in to real-estate, actually that's exactly what they are in. What I meant was, if they began opening up real-estate offices and selling houses, what do you think they would look like? They would have many teenagers running the show very efficiently under a well-planned systematized office, and all the offices would follow the same plan, same hours, same commission structures, same signage, and the agents would all have a well laid out Q and A to help them list the property. Whether it would work or not is irrelevant my point is, McDonalds know they are not in the burger business, burgers are their product. They are in the customer service business and they focus on great systems and training. They could carry their business in to any industry and adopt its principles. This is what you need to consider. Turn your focus away from your products or service for the moment, and consider, what is it about your business that makes you unique?

> *If you changed your products or services a little or a lot, would you really change how you sell them that much?*

Whoops almost forgot. The old way of thinking was to take your product or service and look for the best ways of doing business with it.

We need to work out the best way of doing business. Then introduce our products to the business. If you sell cars, your business model should be able to be incorporated nicely in to that of a clothes shop. It all still involves customer service, finding the right product and managing finances.

Know what your business is and then work your products and services in to it.

Remember

Business

32 The death of (Traditional) Marketing

This is a bit of a side step from the book, (like I haven't had a few already) in to the realm of how marketing has changed. I wanted to go over this only because it is so well connected and linked to sales, that it would be a pity to leave it out.

The chapter headline is probably a little heavy for what we are going to cover. Marketing or traditional marketing hasn't really died like the traditional sales person has, but it has changed enough to warrant a serious look see.

So you understand what marketing is, Marketing, is defined as any form of contact you have with the customer. As I mentioned in chapter twenty eight, the stickers on your car, your clothing, your answering message, TV adds, the products or services themselves, even for better or worse the word of mouth. Every point of customer contact is marketing.

There are five main areas of change in the marketing model we studied last century.

1, Traditionally we would need lots of money for marketing.

The old business model for marketing was to run add campaigns free seminars and giveaways. Now we can use YouTube and Face Book, we can email and we can write blogs. There are many ways to do marketing campaigns for little money if any at all.

2, Marketing used to be a specialized and mysterious trade that the marketing person would have covered.

We now know that marketing is the responsibility of each and every person at the business. As I mentioned, every point of contact a customer has with your business is marketing.

3, We used to measure marketing results by the sales it generated.

We now know we need to measure the bottom line results or profits. Sales figures can lie to us and they can play tricks with the accountant. If sales for the month have increased by five thousand dollars, that's great, but not if the marketing campaign runs up a bill of ten thousand dollars. Treat marketing as a normal business expense and a raw material added to the total cost of what you do.

4,Traditional marketing was a more of a scatter gun approach.

We now know how to focus our efforts much better than we could in the past.

We can search for very specialized demographics like never before.

If you are looking for overweight single mothers with one eye, one leg and blond hair, there will be a database you will be able to access to find these hotties.

5, We now focus our products on those demographics much better.

Lets say you find your one eyed limping mums, and you sell diet pills. Traditionally we would focus on all the overweight ones, (like they haven't got enough problems already). We now understand, women who buy diet products regularly, are far more likely to buy a similar type product again. The same is for men and tools or kids and sporting goods.

Marketing has changed in many other ways, but these are the big ones.
A little research in this area will save you a lot of time and money in the future of your marketing.
Anyone involved in sales should do training in marketing and likewise for marketing people and sales training.

Remember,
Marketing.

33 Time is money?

It was Benjamin Franklin who first said "Remember that time is money."

I'm sure others said it before him, as it's not as profound as we may think. The 1700s (Franklin lived 1706 – 1790) was an all time consuming era.

We were never taught to manage, or allocate our time, or our money for that matter.

Everything needed for the survival of your family took far more time than it does today. Just getting a loaf of bread was half a day's work.

Provided they had grown the wheat. They could grind the grain to get the flour. Then they had to go out and gather the rest of the ingredients such as the milk, from the cows, the lard, the salt, the sugar, and the water from the well, if it was clean enough.
The bread was then baked in an oven beside the fireplace, if there was cut wood to burn.

The average wage in the 1700s was 20p a day (there wasn't much inflation back then, less greed and all), and a loaf of bread was 10p. So in Franklin's era, the average wage would be able to buy two loafs of bread a day. This is fair trade for something that takes half a day to make. Today's average wage will buy fifty loaves a day. And if we want we could also set ourselves up to bake fifty loaves of bread, with all the technology we have like mixers and bread makers.

What does this mean? It means today we no longer need to work for food. Knowing back in the 1700's we would have to work for four days of the week for the household's food supply and two days for clothing and shelter. Today that would mean $800 a week in food. In an age of abundance, we now work for choices.

We will not go hungry if we miss a few days' work, and we will not get cold because the wood is all gone.

What's this got to do with sales? I'm getting to it, just chill McGill

The saying time is money related to a time when we translated everything we earned in to our family's survival. Not much has changed in the way the economy revolves. Essentially we still exchange hours for money, so at a glance you may think the 'time is money' saying still stands.

What has changed in the last few decades is what we can get for the money.

Essentially, whatever we want!

> *The phrase time is money was coined in a century when money was so valuable, four hours of it would be contributed to a loaf of bread.*

The phrase time is money was coined in a century when money was so valuable, four hours of it would be contributed to a loaf of bread, and it wasn't Helga's.

Now we can work for one day in seven and maintain a standard of living higher than there was fifty years ago.

Time is not money anymore. Time is far more valuable than money.

We don't need the money as much as we did then. We can get what we need for a relatively small amount of work, and then we can choose what we want with the rest.

Working for money used to mean, time spent on survival and your family's survival. Now we are constantly being reminded, we need to spend more and more time with our loved ones. Time is not money anymore. Time is what we are all wanting more off.

"This is your life, and it's disappearing one second at a time". Jack, Fight Club. (Jack is Edwards's character, so now ya know).

Time is far more valuable than money.

> *We have the survival thing down, so now we need to move on.*

If we can get a hold of this understanding and know that the 'time is money' is a three hundred year old saying, we can begin to work towards less hours spent for money and more focus on freedom and choices, and those choices with the correct time management will give us the time we want. We have the survival thing down, so now we need to move on. Time is more valuable than money.

Aaaand this relates to sales?

Oh yeah. Do this. For the next twenty one days (takes twenty one days to make or break a habit).

Every time you are planning a run, a day's calls or meetings, consider this chapter, and that whatever you are going to do, your time is worth more than the money it will bring.

I'll say that again, your time is more valuable than the money it will bring. If you keep this thought for a three week period. You will begin to work towards planning a smarter work day. Like I said in the chapter about not being the hardest worker in the office. Chris Gardner found a way to make the same amount of phone calls or more in the valuable time he had. Every day I am looking for ways to do the same job or better in less time.

If you are driving, turn off the radio and listen to educational audio books.

If you are flying or on a train, read.

Time is more valuable than anything on earth. Anything else we can stop using up.

Time is more valuable than money

Remember

Time

34 The new way

Over the last thirty three chapters, we have gone over many old school strategies and new ways of thinking. This chapter will be dedicated to both summarizing and refining the key methods you will need to become the leader in sales your industry is looking for.

I'll start off by saying good job to you for getting through the book without saying "I know what works best" and chucking it.

Also really think about cleaning out the mental bookshelf for this chapter. You will need a completely open mind for the filling up on this one.

Picture this. Close your eyes and, um, that won't work. Just imagine as you're reading. You are sitting opposite the biggest potential client you have ever had the privilege of doing business with. They are powerfully wealthy, and have at least three of your competitors sniffing around and waiting in line to do business with them. For you this would be the career boost you and your company are looking for. There is only one problem, you have forgotten your pants. Kidding. You don't know the person and they don't know you. This meeting was arranged at a convention and they have been put in touch with you to see if there is a chance of a deal being made.

To make matters worse, the person sitting opposite you has a neck tie on with the repeated words 'I hate salesmen' all over it in plain sight.

You also remember them from a news report one evening several months ago, 'lone survivor father of three, loses wife and kids to a rampaging salesman.'

Too much?

You get the picture, this guy is going to be a tough sell. I'm going to show you six things in this book that will give you a basic system to follow, a set of principles needed for the sale to take place, and keep taking place, no matter the customer.

The good thing is, it's all the stuff you have been reading in those thirty three chapters.

Although I said at the beginning of the book, trust was the foundation, you do not have to start with trust. It's actually hard to start building trust unless you already know them, so we need to begin with what we know, and what the customer is looking for. They need help, and they need it in many different ways, most of which they are not aware of. To begin, we need to get their attention.

Marketing.

Your business begins and ends with marketing, and getting your product or service known is the first step. Marketing is the business partner of sales, and should always operate with the end sale in mind. The first question we ask when planning a sales campaign is what do we want at achieve? Remember to keep in mind every piece of communication we have with the customer is a form of marketing. Even a sales rep is a walking talking marketing campaign. So why do we do marketing? The answer should be, to generate interest.

Interest.

If your marketing is done well, you will have the required response from genuinely interested people. From that we can find out what made them interested in the first place. What exactly are they looking for in our range, what can we do for them? In other words, what do they really need?

Need.

Once we have asked a few questions to find out what they particularly need, we then work towards what we can offer them. Their actual need may be a long way from the original marketing that brought them in initially. Ever gone to a shop to get a widget and walked out with a gadget. Our skills and knowledge in the industry will be able to provide the necessary line of questioning to find out what they need. It is then we can offer our insight.

Insight.

Our insight is the customers measuring stick they will use to judge how well we will be able to service them, support them and help them overcome the issues they never knew they had.

This insight we provide will be the conveyer of our technical knowledge data base, combined with our industry knowledge. Insight will be the trust and admiration builder. For the most part, Insight is knowing what questions to ask and how to interpret the answers.

Remember, they are not looking for information, they can get that anywhere. What they are looking for is why X, will work better for them than Y, or Z, and what that will mean for them in the future.

Insight is like a sheriff's badge or certificate of competency. Insight is our best and only real way of letting people know we have the skills and knowledge to help them. The next step is to find out why they are looking to buy, even if they aren't aware they are looking.

Reason.

The reason is the customers 'why' or 'motivation'. To find out the real reasons people buy, we need to look a little deeper. Say for example I want a new car, a nice new sporty black Jag. I want this because I want to be seen in a Jag, and people will want to ride with me, and I may even get in to a club, or a group. I will have more respect than I do now by driving the old bomb I have. I will feel more loved. Like I did when you first got a new toy and all the other kids wanted to play with me, and I want that feeling again. That feeling that people like and want me. I want that feeling because I'm a little lonely.

That's a long way from a new car.

I cannot stress enough, the importance of finding out ones motivation. Knowing the customers reason, will give you such an advantage in the sale, it will make it virtually indestructible. The customer's motivation for buying is your emotional thread to the product or sale. In chapter eighteen I talked about a parent wanting to go to Paris to save their child's life. This is a positive motivation.

There are also negative motivations. I used to be a firm believer in using positive or love as a motivation. All the books I have read and the training I have done points to the positive for a solid motivation. I have since come to understand the opposite. A negative, or a fear will motivate much better than a positive or a love. The fear of loss for example, is very much stronger than the love of a gain. If you want a thousand dollars, you will be willing to do a certain amount of work for that money. If however, you have already got a thousand dollars. You will work harder to keep it. Fear of loss.

We are all better at insuring than we are at saving.

In the business world, you will have a better result finding out what they want to keep, like save their money, or clients. Than you will simply telling them what they will get or gain. Like a larger range or more customers.

Simply asking 'why' a few times, in your own words of course, will delve in to the real motivation for people.

It's not always the reason you first think.

Accurate.

Once we have the reason, we can get to the guts of what they really need.

Think of it as a focus on the right thing. What color do they want, what are they trading in, why are they considering changing brands. Once we know the nitty-grittys, we can begin to build a plan for them.

Plan.

Having a plan for your customers is like helping them with their life. They will see you have thought about where they are going and what they want. They will trust you to be there for the long haul, knowing they are important to you.

Have a business plan for your customers and they will believe in you to deliver. If you wanted to open a shop in a shopping center you will need to provide a business plan. If you wanted a business loan, the bank would ask for a plan. If you want to form a business partnership with your customers. Offer them a well thought out business plan for what you propose to sell them and they will immediately show their admiration for your forethought and business sense.

Solution.

The word solution is thrown around in the corporate world all too freely. If you google the phrase "The solution", you will see it is the catch phrase for thousands of company's around the world. A solution is not an idea for a customer. It's not an offer to them. It's the thing they need like heart surgery. It's the one and only, well planned, educated, home-worked and researched solution that will help them get what they really need, and you are the only one to implement it correctly.

M.I.N.I-R.A.P.S

35 Conclusion

Sales can be both the toughest and the easiest job in the world. It can drive you crazy and at the same time make you fist pump in your car at the traffic lights.

It's been said the life of a soldier is a life of boredom with moments of terror. A role in sales is comparable in many ways. The hours on the road, the waiting and the travel. Then the times when you are faced with such emotional highs and lows as public rejection, humiliation and fear. I have been so scared to visit a prospect that I have postponed or even not called on them for the fear of being rejected or shot

> *The only real choice we ever have in life is the only one that no one can ever take away from us, it is the choice we have to feel how we want about anything that happens to us.*

down. Yet I have risked my life many times over the years. From joining the Army, skydiving and even swimming a kilometer in the middle of the Pacific Ocean to reach a fishing trawler for rescue of our own trawler. None of which even came close to what I have felt while being on the road in the world of sales. Tears, shaking and sleepless nights, all in the name of sales. If you have been in sales for some years already then I salute you for your tenacity. If you are just starting out then I salute you for your spirit.

It all comes down to this, how you perceive what the prospects and customers throw at you. When I joined the Army, I was sent to recruit course. The very first week I remember sitting on my bed thinking I was in the wrong place, what was I doing there in that place? I felt like crap and I thought all the corporals and sergeants hated me. Then I realized all the other recruits had the same look on their faces and where mumbling similar demoralized words to themselves as they sat on their beds. This was their play, this was all a part of the mind games to see who could stand up to the pressure. The only real choice we ever have in life is the only one that no one can ever take away from us, it is the choice we have to feel how we want about anything that happens to us. I changed from I can't handle this to, I am going to get over this and become a soldier.

If you line ten people up and tell each of them they are losers, they will all have entirely different reactions. This is the way they choose to feel, and it is hard but we can fight against it. Just like we can fight against our past training in sales. We will be told we are idiots and just another slimy sales person, but if we can just a little at a time, truly believe we are the most important part of a functional society, we will begin to convey that to our customers with our body language and professional insight, trust and partnership we will develop. And yes we are the most important part of a functional society. It is the oldest profession after all, I know you think something else is the oldest profession, well that also needed to be sold, did it not?

Consider how you feel about what you do. Without you, people just might buy the wrong thing. The world needs good sales professionals to set the record straight, so start acting like a professional.

You are a consultant and a teacher.

You are a guidance counselor and an adviser.

You are the one people will call when they are lost.

As Megatron became Galvatron and Jean Grey, the Phoenix

You have died as a salesperson, and have now risen as Sales Servicemen and Servicewomen.

You are a guide. Brought back to life to teach the new world of customer management, marketing and sales integrity.

References

The Greatest Salesman in the World;
Og Mandino, Bantam Books 1968

Drive & A Whole New Mind; Daniel H Pink. Riverhead Publishing 2009 & 2005

Guerrilla Marketing; Jay Conrad Levinson, Jeannie Levinson, Amy Levinson; *Mariner Books* 1984

Turbostrategy; The Psychology of Selling; The art of closing the Sale;
Brian Tracy 2003 & 1995 Thomas Nelson; 2007

Adapt; Tim Harford, Abacus (Little Brown Book Group) 2011.

Copyright © 2002-2014 Lulu Press, Inc. All Rights Reserved.

www.ingramcontent.com/pod-product-compliance
Lightning Source LLC
Chambersburg PA
CBHW060854170526
45158CB00001B/345